TASTE
LONDON

AUGUST 2024 · GLOBAL EDITION · WWW.TASTEOF.LONDON

A Summer Guide to the Best Bars and Restaurants

LONDON'S COCKTAIL CULTURE

DINING DESTINATIONS
CHONGQING
THE MADERA FABER
QUILON
THE MUNICH CRICKET CLUB
MACELLAIO RC
ROYAL CHINA
CAFE PACIFICO
BABUR
LAZEEZ

MEDIA, YOU AND YOUR BUSINESS

OUTSIDE LONDON
SHOZNA

PIZZA
GORDOS
LISSOME

CHINESE
THE OLD ST CHINESE
YEYE LONDON

CAFE
ARCHES
DORSET

Taste London's Top Tables

THE LEDBURY

127 Ledbury Rd, London W11 2AQ

"The vibes were warm and cozy. Interior was bright. Decorations were thoughtful."

– Katerina Monti

https://theledbury.com

+44 20 7792 9090

CORE BY CLARE SMYTH

92 Kensington Park Rd, London W11 2PN

"Honestly, this is one of my most memorable and amazing meals that I've had."

– Rob L.

https://corebyclaresmyth.com

+44 20 3937 5086

DINNER BY HESTON BLUMENTHAL

66 Knightsbridge, London SW1X 7LA

"The food was delicious and beautifully presented, living up to its Michelin-star reputation."

– Readers' Favorite

https://www.dinnerbyheston.com

+44 20 7201 3833

SKETCH

9 Conduit St, London W1S 2XG

"Incredible lunch at the lecture room. Exquisite food/ decor/hospitality/service."

– Sums S.

https://sketch.london

+44 20 7659 4500

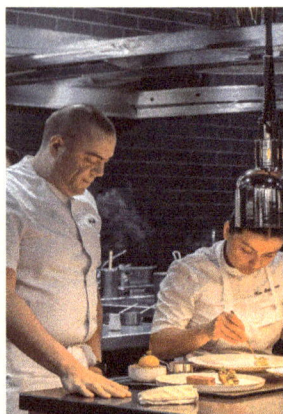

GORDON RAMSAY

68 Royal Hospital Rd, London SW3 4HPA

"To say the food here is amazing is probably an understatement."

– Prashant Gandhi

https://gordonramsayrestaurants.com

+44 20 7352 4441

THE CLOVE CLUB

380 Old Street, London EC1V 9LT

"Had an enjoyable evening at the bar counter for single diner."

– Guanny G.

https://www.thecloveclub.com

+44 20 7729 6496

LYLE'S

656 Shoreditch High St, London E1 6JJ

"A lovely atmosphere with the service to match."

– Nikola Sariyski

https://www.lyleslondon.com/

+44 20 3011 5911

A. WONG

70 Wilton Rd, Pimlico, London SW1V 1DE

"The food was absolutely incredible - a banquet of tiny, perfect dishes representing the 8 culinary styles of Chinese cooking."

– Rebecca Magnus

https://www.awong.co.uk

+44 20 7828 8931

Indulge in London's Finest Flavours

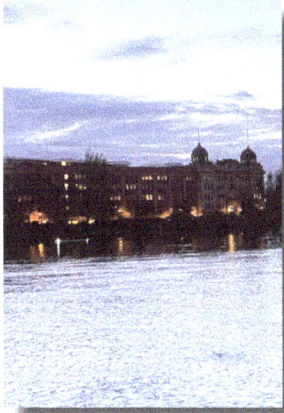

THE RIVER CAFÉ

Rainville Rd, London W6 9HA

"A very busy and popular restaurant. They pack a lot of diners into the space and limit your table to two hours."

– Stuart Cooke

https://www.rivercafe.co.uk/

+44 20 7386 4200

LE GAVROCHE

43 Upper Brook St, London W1K 7QR

"An amazing experience!"

– Simon Nutt

https://www.le-gavroche.co.uk

+44 20 7408 0881

AMAYA

Motcomb St, London SW1X 8JT

"What an experience! Food was stellar, service excellent."

– Robin Rocks

https://www.amaya.biz

+44 20 7823 1166

GYMKHANA

42 Albemarle St, London W1S 4JH

"One of the best meals we have ever had."

– Sean Phillips

https://gymkhanalondon.com

+44 20 3011 5900

TRISHNA

15-17 Blandford St, London, W1U 3DG

"The food was exquisite, and the masterful use of spices elevated each dish to another level!"

– Karen Wood

https://www.trishnalondon.com

+44 20 7935 5624

BRAT

4 Redchurch St, London E1 6JL

"The atmosphere was relaxed but great to see the open kitchen and watch the food being prepped."

– Dominic Michaelis

https://bratrestaurant.co.uk

+44 20 3011 1800

IKOYI

180 Strand, Temple, London WC2R 1EA

"Oh Wow oh wow!"

– Debs Lister

https://ikoyilondon.com

+44 20 3583 4660

LOUIE

13-15 West St, London WC2H 9NE

"Everything was amazing. From the ambiance, to the New Orleans cuisine to the service..."

– Crispy Cakes

https://louie-london.com

+44 20 8057 1100

IN THIS ISSUE

EDITOR'S LETTER

Published by
Newyox Media Ltd.
200 Suite
134-146 Curtain Road
EC2A 3AR London
t: +44 20 3695 0809
whatsapp at +44 79 3847 8420
editor@tasteof.london
https://tasteof.london

George Shaw
Editor-In-Chief
editor@tasteof.londonm

A. Baldie
Managing Editor

Binod Barad
Restaurant Advisor

Dan Peters
Review Editor
writer@ tasteof.london

Review Writers
Charlotte Burrows
Geneviève Grant
Lesley McHarg
George Shaw
Kirsity Row
Storm Greenwood
Giulia Carla Rossi

CONTRIBUTOS
Cumba Gowri
Sridevi Balamurugan
Bhavesh B
Adrian T. Cheng
Anselm Ianyoha
Shalini M
Chowdhury Shaid-Uz-Zaman
Lyne Evans
State Point
Tony GraysonJon Allo
Oladimeji Ajegbile

Dear Readers,

We are thrilled to present the seventh issue of Taste London, marking our return after a brief hiatus. As we dive back into the vibrant culinary scene of this incredible city, we are committed to bringing you the most comprehensive reviews of London's best and coziest restaurants and cafes. This summer, we are accelerating our efforts to explore and share the hidden gems and renowned establishments that make London a gastronomic paradise.

Taste London magazine is available in both print and electronic formats, accessible online and through social media. We take pride in being one of the rare British magazines available in print across over 190 countries and more than 40,000 retail platforms and online stores, including Amazon, Barnes & Noble, Waterstones, Blackwells, and Walmart.

You might think that running a local business means you only need to reach local people. However, that's not entirely true. Our magazine serves a dual purpose for restaurants. Firstly, millions of tourists visit London each year, and they often research their dining options before their trip begins. Therefore, having a global reach is crucial. Secondly, featuring your restaurant in our magazine means your establishment is introduced to a global market with metadata that significantly boosts your SEO efforts. In short, our magazine can greatly enhance your marketing strategy by ensuring your restaurant's name is included as keywords in our metadata.

This issue's cover story is "A Summer Guide to the Best Bars and Restaurants - London's Cocktail Culture." We have curated a list of some of the finest cocktail bars and restaurants for you, a task that was both challenging and delightful given the plethora of options available.

Our food critique experts have visited and reviewed some of London's best and coziest restaurants, sharing their thoughts on the food and ambiance. The featured restaurants in this issue include:

- Chongqing
- The Madera
- Faber
- Quilon
- The Munich Cricket Club
- Macellaio RC
- Shozna
- Royal China
- Cafe Pacifico
- Babur
- Lazeez
- Lissome
- YeYe's
- Gordo's Pizza
- The Old Street Chinese 46
- Arches Cafe

Additionally, we have enclosed a must-read article for restaurant owners titled "Media, You and Your Business: Effective Media Strategies for Your Restaurant." This 7-minute read is packed with valuable insights to help you leverage media for your business success.

If you believe your restaurant is among the best and coziest in this vibrant city, we invite you to contact us for a review.

Enjoy reading, and thank you for being a part of our culinary journey.

George Shaw
Editor-in-Chief
Taste London Magazine

A Summer Guide to the Best Bars and Restaurants

LONDON'S COCKTAIL CULTURE

Explore London's vibrant cocktail scene this summer, featuring classic and innovative drinks at top bars and restaurants like The Connaught Bar, Nightjar, and The Alchemist. Cheers to Experience the magic of mixology with this stunning cocktail.

As the summer sun graces the streets of London, there's no better time to explore the city's vibrant cocktail scene. London, a melting pot of cultures and flavours, offers an array of cocktail bars and restaurants that cater to every palate. Whether you're a fan of classic concoctions or innovative mixes, the city's cocktail culture is sure to impress. Here's a guide to understanding and appreciating cocktails in London, along with a sneak peek into some of the best spots to enjoy them.

The Art of Cocktails

Cocktails are more than just drinks; they are a blend of art and science. The perfect cocktail balances flavours, aromas, and textures, creating a sensory experience that goes beyond mere refreshment. In London, bartenders, often referred to as mixologists, take pride in their craft, using high-quality ingredients and innovative techniques to create drinks that are both delicious and visually stunning.

Classic Cocktails with a Twist

London's cocktail bars are known for their ability to reinvent classic cocktails. Take the Martini, for example. While the traditional gin or vodka Martini remains a favorite, many bars offer unique variations, such as the Espresso Martini, which combines vodka, coffee liqueur, and espresso for a rich, caffeinated kick. Another popular twist is the Elderflower Collins, a refreshing take on the Tom Collins, featuring gin, elderflower liqueur, lemon juice, and soda water.

Innovative Mixes

For those who crave something new, London's cocktail scene does not disappoint. Bars like The Alchemist and Nightjar are renowned for their experimental drinks. The Alchemist, for instance, offers cocktails that bubble, smoke, and change color, providing a theatrical drinking experience. Nightjar, on the other hand, is famous for its vintage-inspired cocktails, often incorporating rare and unusual ingredients.

The Perfect Summer Cocktails

Summer in London calls for light, refreshing cocktails that can be enjoyed in the city's many outdoor spaces. The Aperol Spritz, with its vibrant orange hue and bittersweet taste, is a summer staple. Made with Aperol, Prosecco, and a splash of soda, it's the perfect drink for a sunny afternoon. Another summer favorite is the Mojito, a Cuban classic made with rum, fresh mint, lime juice, sugar, and soda water. Its crisp, minty flavor is incredibly refreshing on a hot day.

London's cocktail culture is a testament to the city's creativity and diversity. Whether you're a local or a visitor, exploring the city's cocktail bars and restaurants is a delightful way to experience London's vibrant nightlife. So, this summer, raise a glass to the art of cocktails and enjoy the best that London has to offer. Cheers!

Experience the magic of mixology with this stunning cocktail.

LONDON'S BEST COCTAIL BARS & RESTAURANTS

The Best Bars and Restaurants

While the list of London's top cocktail bars and restaurants is extensive, here are a few must-visit spots:

THE CONNAUGHT BAR

Known for its elegant setting and expertly crafted cocktails.

"Elegance in every sip at The Connaught Bar, where expertly crafted cocktails meet a sophisticated setting."

LYANESS

Located in the Mondrian Hotel, offering innovative drinks with a botanical twist.

"Discover innovative drinks with a botanical twist at Lyaness, located in the chic Mondrian Hotel."

NIGHTJAR

A speakeasy-style bar with a focus on vintage cocktails.

"Step back in time at Nightjar, a speakeasy-style bar specializing in vintage cocktails."

THE ALCHEMIST

Famous for its theatrical and experimental cocktails.

"Experience the magic of mixology with The Alchemist's theatrical and experimental cocktails."

SWIFT

A two-floor bar with a relaxed atmosphere and a diverse cocktail menu.

"Relax and unwind at Swift, a two-floor bar offering a diverse and delightful cocktail menu."

ORIOLE

An exotic bar with a menu inspired by global flavours.

"Embark on a global flavor journey at Oriole, an exotic bar with a world-inspired cocktail menu."

BAR TERMINI

A small, Italian-style bar known for its Negronis.

"Savour the classic charm of Bar Termini, a small Italian-style bar renowned for its Negronis."

CALLOOH CALLAY

A quirky bar with a playful cocktail menu.

"Indulge in playful and quirky cocktails at Callooh Callay, where creativity knows no bounds."

HAPPINESS FORGETS

A basement bar with a cozy, intimate vibe.

"Find cozy, intimate vibes and exceptional drinks at Happiness Forgets, a hidden basement gem."

69 COLEBROOKE ROW

Also known as The Bar With No Name, offering sophisticated cocktails in a minimalist setting.

"Enjoy sophisticated cocktails in a minimalist setting at 69 Colebrooke Row, also known as The Bar With No Name."

THREE SHEETS

A minimalist bar with a focus on high-quality ingredients.

"Experience the art of simplicity at Three Sheets, a minimalist bar focused on high-quality ingredients."

For those who crave something new, London's cocktail scene does not disappoint. Bars like The Alchemist and Nightjar are renowned for their experimental drinks.

LONDON'S BEST COCTAIL BARS & RESTAURANTS

THE CONNAUGHT BAR

The Connaught Bar in Mayfair, London, is renowned for its chic and innovative cocktails. Signature drinks include the Connaught Martini, crafted with Grey Goose Vodka, Connaught Bar Gin, and Martini Ambrato, enhanced with Amalfi lemon oil and a distillation of five bitters. The bar's menu features timeless classics like the Ristretto Manhattan and champagne cocktails, all served in an ultra-stylish setting.

The Connaught Hotel, 16 Carlos Place, Mayfair, London, W1K 2AL
+44 20 7314 3419
https://www.the-connaught.co.uk
restaurants-bars/connaught-bar

LYANESS

"Lyaness" is a renowned cocktail bar located in London, UK. Formerly known as "Dandelyan," it was rebranded as "Lyaness" in 2018. The bar is famous for its innovative and creative cocktails crafted by award-winning mixologists. Lyaness is known for its unique approach to cocktail creation, using unusual ingredients and techniques to deliver exceptional drinks. If you're a cocktail enthusiast or looking for a memorable drinking experience in London, Lyaness is definitely worth a visit.

20 Upper Ground, South Bank, London SE1 9PD
+44 20 3747 1063
https://www.lyaness.com
lyaness@seacontainerslondon.com

NIGHTJAR

Nightjar, a hidden gem in London's Shoreditch, stands out as one of the best cocktail bars due to its dedication to vintage-inspired mixology and a speakeasy atmosphere. This bar transports guests back to the glamour of the Jazz Age with its dim lighting, live jazz music, and an extensive menu of meticulously crafted cocktails. Nightjar's drinks are a blend of historical recipes and modern innovation, often featuring rare and exotic ingredients. The bar's intimate setting and exceptional service create a unique and memorable experience, making it a top choice for cocktail aficionados.

129 City Road, London EC1V 1JB
+44 20 7253 4101
https://www.barnightjar.com/
info@barnightjar.com

THE ALCHEMIST

The Alchemist is renowned for its theatrical and innovative approach to mixology, making it one of the best cocktail bars. Each drink is a sensory experience, featuring dramatic presentations with smoke, fire, and color-changing concoctions. The bar's commitment to creativity and quality is evident in its extensive menu, which combines classic cocktails with modern twists. The Alchemist's unique ambiance, characterized by a blend of industrial chic and mystical elements, enhances the overall experience. With multiple locations across the UK, The Alchemist consistently delivers exceptional service and unforgettable drinks, solidifying its status as a top destination for cocktail enthusiasts.

6 Bevis Marks, London EC3A 7BA
+44 20 7283 8800
https://thealchemist.uk.com
info@thealchemist.uk.com

SWIFT

Swift, located in the heart of Soho, London, is celebrated for its elegant ambiance and expertly crafted cocktails, making it one of the best cocktail bars. The bar is divided into two distinct areas: the bright and lively upstairs bar, perfect for aperitifs and lighter drinks, and the cozy, intimate downstairs bar, ideal for savoring more complex and sophisticated cocktails. Swift's menu is a testament to the art of mixology, featuring a range of classic and contemporary drinks made with high-quality ingredients. The bar's knowledgeable and friendly staff provide exceptional service, ensuring a memorable experience for every guest. Swift's combination of stylish decor, innovative cocktails, and warm hospitality makes it a must-visit destination for cocktail lovers.

12 Old Compton Street, Soho, London W1D 4TQ
+44 20 7437 7820
https://www.barswift.com
info@barswift.com

ORIOLE

Oriole, located in Smithfield Market, London, is widely regarded as one of the best cocktail bars due to its exotic and adventurous approach to mixology. The bar's interior is inspired by the golden age of exploration, featuring lush, tropical decor that transports guests to far-flung destinations. Oriole's cocktail menu is a journey in itself, offering a diverse selection of drinks that draw inspiration from around the world. Each cocktail is meticulously crafted with unique ingredients and presented with artistic flair. The bar also hosts live music performances, adding to the vibrant and immersive atmosphere. Oriole's dedication to creativity, quality, and exceptional service makes it a standout destination for cocktail enthusiasts seeking a truly unique experience.

East Poultry Avenue, Smithfield Markets, London EC1A 9LH
+44 20 3457 8099
https://www.oriolebar.com
info@oriolebar.com

Bar Termini

Bar Termini, located in the heart of Soho, London, is renowned for its Italian-inspired cocktails and intimate, stylish setting. This small but perfectly formed bar is a tribute to the classic Italian café culture, offering a refined yet relaxed atmosphere. Bar Termini's menu is a masterclass in simplicity and elegance, featuring expertly crafted cocktails that highlight the finest Italian ingredients and techniques. The bar is particularly famous for its Negronis, which are served in a variety of innovative twists. In addition to its exceptional drinks, Bar Termini also offers a selection of Italian aperitifs and small plates, making it an ideal spot for a pre-dinner drink or a leisurely evening out. The combination of impeccable service, high-quality cocktails, and a charming ambiance makes Bar Termini a must-visit destination for cocktail aficionados.

7 Old Compton Street, Soho, London W1D 5JE
+44 20 7437 2525
https://www.bar-termini.com
drinks@bar-termini.com

Callooh Callay

Callooh Callay, located in the vibrant Shoreditch area of London, is celebrated for its whimsical and eclectic approach to cocktails and bar design. Named after a line from Lewis Carroll's "Jabberwocky," the bar embraces a playful and imaginative theme that sets it apart from more traditional cocktail venues. The interior is a delightful mix of quirky decor, hidden rooms, and unexpected surprises, creating an atmosphere that is both fun and sophisticated.

Callooh Callay's cocktail menu is as inventive as its decor, featuring a rotating selection of creative drinks that push the boundaries of mixology. The bar staff are known for their expertise and passion, ensuring that each cocktail is crafted to perfection. Whether you're looking for a classic drink with a twist or something entirely new and experimental, Callooh Callay delivers an unforgettable experience.

65 Rivington Street, Shoreditch, London EC2A 3AY
+44 20 7739 4781
https://www.calloohcallaybar.com
info@calloohcallaybar.com

Happiness Forgets

Happiness Forgets, nestled in the trendy Hoxton Square of London, is a hidden gem known for its unpretentious yet sophisticated approach to cocktails. This basement bar exudes a cozy, intimate vibe, making it a perfect spot for those who appreciate high-quality drinks in a relaxed setting. Despite its understated appearance, Happiness Forgets has garnered a reputation for excellence, often being listed among the best bars in the world.

The bar's philosophy is simple: great cocktails without the fuss. The menu features a curated selection of classic and contemporary drinks, all crafted with precision and care by a team of skilled bartenders. The focus is on balance and flavor, ensuring that each cocktail is a memorable experience. The knowledgeable staff are always on hand to recommend drinks based on your preferences, adding a personal touch to your visit.

Happiness Forgets is also known for its welcoming and inclusive atmosphere. The dim lighting, comfortable seating, and friendly service create a space where guests can unwind and enjoy their drinks without any pretension. It's a place where both cocktail connoisseurs and casual drinkers can feel at home.

8-9 Hoxton Square, Hoxton, London N1 6NU
+44 20 7613 0325
https://www.happinessforgets.com
info@happinessforgets.com

69 COLEBROOKE ROW

69 Colebrooke Row, also known as "The Bar With No Name," is a renowned cocktail bar located in the heart of Islington, London. This intimate and stylish venue has earned a stellar reputation for its innovative drinks and exceptional service, making it a favorite among cocktail enthusiasts and industry professionals alike.

The bar is the brainchild of Tony Conigliaro, a pioneering mixologist known for his experimental approach to cocktail creation. At 69 Colebrooke Row, the focus is on pushing the boundaries of traditional mixology, using cutting-edge techniques and high-quality ingredients to craft unique and memorable drinks. The menu features a mix of classic cocktails and original creations, each meticulously designed to deliver a perfect balance of flavours.

Despite its small size, 69 Colebrooke Row has made a big impact on the cocktail scene, frequently appearing on lists of the best bars in the world. Its commitment to innovation and quality has earned it a loyal following and numerous accolades.

69 Colebrooke Row, Islington, London N1 8AA

+44 20 7354 9993

https://www.69colebrookerow.com

info@69colebrookerow.com

THREE SHEETS

Three Sheets, located in the vibrant neighborhood of Dalston, London, is a standout cocktail bar known for its minimalist approach and expertly crafted drinks. This bar, run by the talented Venning brothers, has quickly become a favorite among locals and visitors alike, thanks to its innovative menu and welcoming atmosphere.

The philosophy at Three Sheets is all about simplicity and quality. The bar features a concise menu of cocktails, each one thoughtfully designed to highlight a few key ingredients. This approach allows the flavours to shine and ensures that every drink is perfectly balanced. The menu is divided into three sections—Light & Fresh, Medium & Balanced, and Rich & Bold—making it easy for guests to find a cocktail that suits their mood and preferences.

What sets Three Sheets apart is its commitment to excellence in every aspect. The bartenders are highly skilled and passionate about their craft, always ready to share their knowledge and make recommendations. The bar itself is sleek and modern, with a relaxed and unpretentious vibe that makes it a great spot for both casual drinks and special occasions.

Three Sheets has received numerous accolades and is often listed among the best bars in London. Its dedication to quality, innovation, and hospitality has earned it a loyal following and a reputation as a must-visit destination for cocktail lovers.

510b Kingsland Road, Dalston, London E8 4AB

+44 20 7249 0472

https://www.threesheets-bar.com

info@threesheets-bar.com

COUPETTE

Coupette, located in the lively neighborhood of Bethnal Green, London, is a celebrated cocktail bar known for its French-inspired drinks and chic, relaxed atmosphere. Since its opening, Coupette has garnered a reputation for excellence, making it a go-to destination for cocktail enthusiasts and industry professionals.

The bar was founded by Chris Moore, a renowned mixologist with a passion for French culture and flavours. This influence is evident in Coupette's menu, which features a range of innovative cocktails that incorporate classic French ingredients and techniques. One of the bar's signature drinks, the "Champagne Piña Colada," has become iconic for its unique twist on a tropical favorite, using French cider instead of the traditional rum.

In addition to its outstanding cocktails, Coupette also offers a selection of fine wines and spirits, with a particular focus on French products. This dedication to authenticity and quality has earned Coupette numerous awards and a place on many lists of the best bars in the world.

423 Bethnal Green Road, Bethnal Green, London E2 0A

+44 20 7729 5692

https://www.coupette.co.uk

info@coupette.co.uk

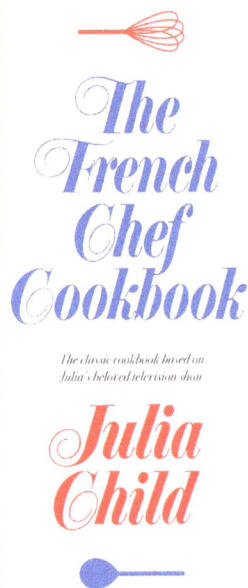

THE FRENCH CHEF COOKBOOK
by Julia Child

MELİZ'S KITCHEN
by Meliz Berg

THE NEW BASICS COOKBOOK
by Sheila Lukins

Julia Child's "The French Chef Cookbook" is a timeless culinary masterpiece, making French cuisine accessible, delightful, and inspiring for all.

The French Chef Cookbook by Julia Child is a timeless culinary classic that continues to inspire both novice and experienced cooks alike. This cookbook, which is a companion to her groundbreaking television series "The French Chef," encapsulates the essence of French cooking in a way that is accessible and engaging.

The book is meticulously organized, with each recipe presented in a clear and concise manner. Julia Child's unique voice and personality shine through in her detailed instructions and helpful tips. The recipes are accompanied by anecdotes and insights that make the cooking process enjoyable and educational.

The recipes in *The French Chef Cookbook* range from simple to complex, catering to a wide array of skill levels. Whether you're looking to master the art of making a perfect omelette or tackle the more challenging Coq au Vin, this cookbook provides the guidance needed to achieve culinary success. The step-by-step instructions are easy to follow, and the inclusion of ingredient substitutions and variations adds flexibility for home cooks.

The French Chef Cookbook is more than just a collection of recipes; it is a piece of culinary history. Julia Child's influence on American cooking is undeniable, and this book serves as a testament to her passion for food and education. It is a must-have for any cook interested in exploring the rich traditions of French cuisine.

The French Chef Cookbook by Julia Child is a valuable addition to any kitchen library. Its comprehensive and user-friendly approach makes it an essential resource for anyone looking to expand their culinary repertoire. Julia Child's legacy lives on through this cookbook, inspiring generations of cooks to embrace the joys of French cooking.

"Meliz's Kitchen" is a beautifully crafted cookbook, offering delicious, authentic Turkish-Cypriot recipes with easy-to-follow instructions and stunning photos.

Meliz's Kitchen by Meliz Berg is a delightful culinary journey into the heart of Turkish-Cypriot cuisine. This cookbook is a treasure trove of comforting and authentic recipes that bring the rich flavors and traditions of Turkish-Cypriot food right into your home kitchen.

One of the standout features of this book is its accessibility. The recipes are straightforward and easy to follow, making it perfect for both novice cooks and seasoned chefs looking to explore new culinary horizons. Meliz Berg's clear instructions and helpful tips ensure that even complex dishes are manageable.

The book is beautifully presented, with vibrant photographs that not only showcase the delicious dishes but also capture the essence of Turkish-Cypriot culture. Each recipe is accompanied by a personal anecdote or cultural insight, adding a warm and personal touch that makes the book feel like a conversation with a friend.

The variety of recipes is impressive, ranging from hearty mains to delectable desserts. Whether you're in the mood for a comforting bowl of Kıymalı Garavolli (minced lamb and pasta) or a sweet treat like Baklava, "Meliz's Kitchen" has something to satisfy every craving. The emphasis on fresh, wholesome ingredients ensures that the dishes are not only tasty but also nourishing.

What sets this cookbook apart is its ability to evoke nostalgia and create new memories. Many readers have shared how the recipes brought back fond memories of family meals and childhood flavors. It's a testament to Meliz Berg's skill in capturing the soul of Turkish-Cypriot cuisine and making it accessible to a global audience.

Meliz's Kitchen is a must-have for anyone interested in exploring the rich culinary traditions of Cyprus and Turkey. It's a beautifully crafted book that promises to bring warmth, flavor, and a touch of Mediterranean sunshine to your kitchen. Highly recommended!

"The New Basics Cookbook" is a timeless treasure, offering diverse, delicious recipes with clear instructions and charming illustrations

The New Basics Cookbook by Sheila Lukins and Julee Rosso is a comprehensive and beloved resource for home cooks. This cookbook, which follows the success of their "Silver Palate" series, offers a wide array of recipes that cater to both everyday meals and special occasions.

With over 875 recipes, this cookbook provides a vast selection of dishes, ensuring that there is something for everyone. From appetizers to desserts, the variety is impressive. The recipes are well-written with detailed instructions, making them accessible even for those who are new to cooking. The step-by-step guidance helps ensure successful results.

Throughout the book, the authors share valuable cooking tips and techniques that can enhance your culinary skills. These insights are particularly beneficial for those looking to improve their cooking. The book features delightful black and white illustrations that add a touch of charm and make it enjoyable to read. Many recipes include serving suggestions, which can help you create balanced and visually appealing meals.

However, some recipes can be quite complex and require a long list of ingredients, which might be overwhelming for beginners. There have also been reports of occasional errors in the recipes. Despite these minor drawbacks, *The New Basics Cookbook* remains a beloved classic that continues to inspire home cooks around the world.

DELICIOUS READS

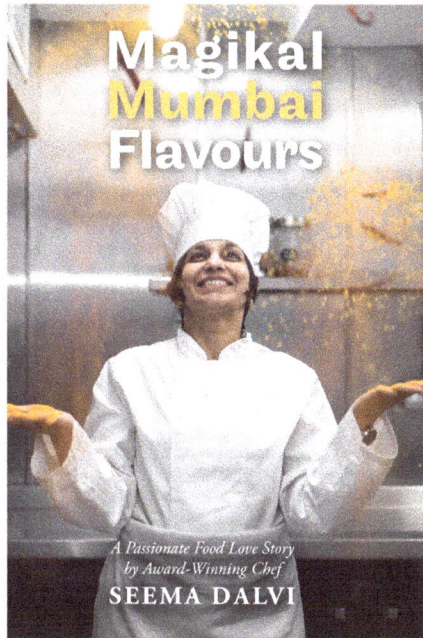

MAGIKAL MUMBAI FLAVOURS:
by Seema Dalvi

EVERY GRAIN OF RICE
by Fuchsia Dunlop

CLEORA'S KITCHENS
by Cleora Butler

Magikal Mumbai Flavours is a captivating culinary journey, blending authentic recipes with rich cultural stories. A must-read for food lovers!

"*Magikal Mumbai Flavours: A Passionate Food Love Story*" by Chef Seema Dalvi is a delightful culinary journey that beautifully intertwines food and culture. This book is not just a collection of recipes; it is a heartfelt narrative that captures the essence of Mumbai's vibrant culinary scene.

The book is meticulously written and features stunning photographs that bring the recipes to life. Each page exudes a personal connection to the dishes, making it evident that Chef Seema Dalvi has poured her heart and soul into this work. The recipes are well-explained, making them accessible to both novice and experienced cooks.

One of the standout features of this book is the section that delves into the cultural significance of the recipes. Chef Seema provides insightful anecdotes and historical context, which enriches the reader's understanding and appreciation of Mumbai's diverse food heritage.

Readers have praised the book for its engaging story-telling and the authenticity of the recipes. The personal touch in the narrative makes it more than just a cookbook; it feels like a journey through Mumbai's bustling streets and aromatic kitchens. The book has received positive reviews for its ability to evoke nostalgia and inspire culinary creativity.

Magikal Mumbai Flavours is a must-have for anyone interested in Indian cuisine and culture. Chef Seema Dalvi has created a masterpiece that not only teaches you how to cook but also tells a passionate story of love for food and tradition. Whether you are a food enthusiast or someone looking to explore new culinary horizons, this book is a treasure trove of flavors and stories waiting to be discovered.

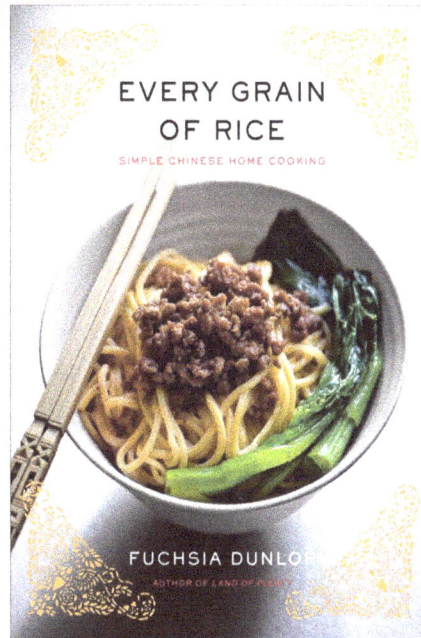

Every Grain of Rice by Fuchsia Dunlop is a culinary treasure, offering simple, authentic Chinese recipes with clear instructions and beautiful photos.

Every Grain of Rice: Simple Chinese Home Cooking by Fuchsia Dunlop is a culinary gem that brings the rich and diverse flavors of Chinese home cooking to your kitchen. As someone who loves exploring different cuisines, I found this book to be an invaluable resource.

The book is beautifully presented with clear, vibrant photographs that make each dish look incredibly appetizing. Dunlop's writing is engaging and informative, providing not just recipes but also insights into Chinese culinary traditions and techniques. This makes the book suitable for both beginners and experienced cooks.

One of the standout features of this cookbook is its focus on simplicity and authenticity. The recipes are straightforward and use ingredients that are relatively easy to find, even if you don't live near a specialty Asian market. This accessibility is a huge plus for home cooks who want to try their hand at Chinese cooking without feeling overwhelmed.

The variety of recipes is impressive, covering everything from hearty soups and stir-fries to delicate dumplings and refreshing salads. Each recipe is well-explained, with step-by-step instructions that are easy to follow. I particularly appreciated the tips on preparation and cooking techniques, which helped me achieve the best results.

Every Grain of Rice is a must-have for anyone interested in Chinese cuisine. It not only provides delicious recipes but also educates and inspires. Whether you're a novice cook or a seasoned chef, this book will undoubtedly become a cherished part of your culinary library.

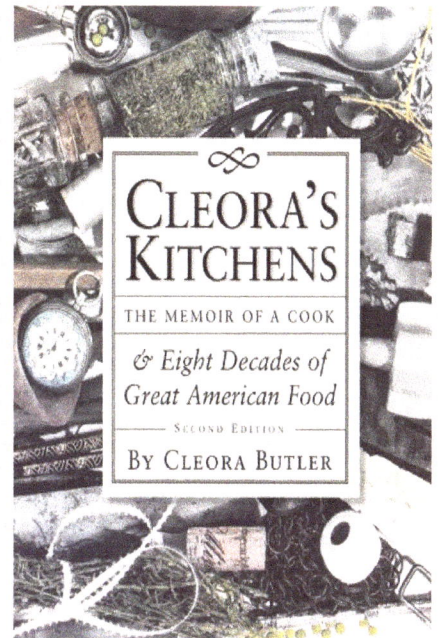

Cleora's Kitchens" beautifully intertwines personal stories and recipes, celebrating African American culinary heritage with warmth and authenticity.

Cleora's Kitchens by Cleora Butler is a captivating blend of memoir and cookbook that offers a unique glimpse into the evolution of American cuisine through the eyes of an African American cook. Spanning eight decades, Butler's narrative begins with her childhood in Texas and follows her journey through various kitchens, capturing the essence of African American culinary traditions and their impact on American food culture.

The book features over 300 recipes, each a testament to Butler's rich culinary heritage and the diverse influences that shaped her cooking. From Southern classics to innovative dishes, the recipes are presented with detailed instructions and personal anecdotes that bring them to life. Butler's storytelling is engaging and heartfelt, providing readers with a deep sense of connection to her experiences and the historical context in which she lived.

Readers have praised "Cleora's Kitchens" for its authenticity and the warmth of Butler's narrative. The memoir is not just a collection of recipes but a journey through history, offering valuable insights into the cultural and social dynamics of the times. The book is enriched with historical tidbits, such as the origins of kitchen staples like graham crackers and food processors, adding an educational layer to the memoir.

Butler's stories are filled with nostalgia and emotion, making the book a compelling read. Her ability to weave personal experiences with culinary history offers a unique perspective on American food culture, particularly the contributions of African American cooks. "Cleora's Kitchens" is a must-read for culinary enthusiasts, history buffs, and anyone interested in the rich tapestry of American cuisine.

In summary, "Cleora's Kitchens" is a beautifully crafted memoir that celebrates the life and legacy of Cleora Butler. It is a valuable resource for preserving and honoring African American culinary traditions, making it a cherished addition to any kitchen library.

TASTE OF CQ

CHONQUING
Culinary Diversity on Every Plate

BY
LESLEY
MCHARG

"Chonquing: a Central London hotspot with oriental charm. Warm hospitality, diverse menu from Sichuan to classics. Peking Duck, a highlight—tableside carving, delightful flavours, and versatile serving. A gem signifying "double happiness.

The dished at Chongqing are a true delight.

Taste of Chongqing Restaurant, nestled in the heart of bustling Central London, is an enchanting gem that promises a delightful culinary journey. Its strategic location near transport hubs caters to both tourists from the neighbouring Royal National Hotel and loyal local patrons. Offering a blend of dine-in and takeaway options, this family-owned establishment exudes an inviting aura from the moment you approach its vibrant exterior.

Stepping inside, the ambiance is a seamless fusion of simplicity and oriental charm. Chinese lanterns and ornaments adorn the ceilings and walls, while the modern wooden dining tables boast convenient features like heated lazy Susans and built-in charging points for tech-savvy diners.

As guests, we discovered the restaurant's exclusive VIP private dining room, a hidden gem offering a secluded and elegant space perfect for intimate gatherings. It comfortably accommodates up to 18 guests, making it an ideal setting for a memorable time with friends and family. The additional karaoke services and other entertainment options were a delightful surprise, promising more fun for our next visit! What adds an extra touch of elegance are the fresh flower arrangements crafted weekly by the dedicated staff, elevating the dining experience to a whole new level.

The warmth of Chonquing extends beyond its decor, resonating through the gracious hospitality of the staff, notably Jessica, a welcoming member of the close-knit family team. With roots stemming from the same province in China and a shared dialect, the team exudes unity and attentiveness, ensuring a personalized and engaging dining experience for each guest.

The menu is a treasure trove for food enthusiasts, boasting a diverse array of dishes ranging from signature plates to Sichuan specialties and an abundance of vegetarian options. The drinks menu complements the culinary offerings with an impressive selection of wines, beverages, beers, and unique Chinese liqueurs, catering to various preferences and budgets.

As for the culinary journey itself, the Sichuan Beef & Onions and the classic Sweet and Sour Chicken with egg fried rice tantalize the taste buds with their flavoursome presentation. The chicken is remarkably crispy, with a delightful balance of sweet and sour flavours – it's a real treat. Tender Beef with Spring Onions, a dish perfect for those who enjoy a hint of spice without overwhelming heat, combines succulent beef with the fragrant aroma of onions. However, the pièce de resistance is the Peking Duck, a standout recommendation from the atten-

tive staff. This Beijing specialty takes centre stage, expertly carved tableside by a chef, delivering a culinary spectacle. The accompaniments—dips, crudités, and sugar—accentuate the duck's flavours, offering a delightful departure from the traditional aromatic duck with pancakes. The versatility of the remaining duck, served as a soup or stir-fry, further enriches this gastronomic adventure.

In essence, Chonquing Restaurant embodies its name's essence—double happiness—by delivering an exquisite dining experience that transcends expectations. With its inviting ambiance, diverse menu, and exceptional service, it's an absolute gem for culinary enthusiasts seeking an unforgettable journey through Chinese cuisine.

THE MADERA

THE FOOD: Absolutely delicious. Beef barbacoa, which was served with avocado crema, gem lettuce, and mango cheese, was tender and flavourfull, and the avocado crema added a nice touch of creaminess.

THE VIEWS: The views from the Madera Restaurant are simply stunning. The restaurant is located on the 15th floor of the Treehouse Hotel, and it offers 360-degree views of the city. On a clear day, you can see all the way to Buckingham Palace and the Houses of Parliament.

THE SERVICE: The service at Madera is excellent. The staff are friendly and attentive, and they are always happy to answer any questions you may have about the menu or the wine list.

THE ATMOSPHERE: The atmosphere at Madera is modern and stylish. The restaurant is decorated in a sleek, contemporary style, and the lighting is soft and inviting. There is also a large outdoor terrace that is perfect for al fresco dining.

PHOTO: The Madera Restaurant offers a vibrant treehouse ambiance with panoramic London views, friendly service, and a unique Mexican menu with a Californian twist for an unforgettable dining experience. Image Courtesy of bacchus.agency

The Madera Offers An Enchanting Dining Experience

BY LESLEY MCHARG

> The ambiance is complemented by modern lighting, decor, and music that cater to both city workers looking for a sophisticated night out and tourists seeking a special dining experience.

Elevate your dining experience at The Madera Restaurant, where chic meets enchanting treehouse vibes high above London's Langham Place.

Nestled atop the Treehouse Hotel in London's Langham Place, The Madera Restaurant offers an enchanting dining experience that starts the moment you ascend from the foliage-filled lift to the 15th floor. This rooftop gem wraps you in a treehouse ambiance that is both chic and inviting, setting the stage for a memorable meal.

Upon arrival, Lawrence, the Restaurant Manager, provided a warm and friendly welcome that set the tone for the exceptional service to come. The staff, attired in smart uniforms, were attentive without being intrusive, ensuring a comfortable and well-cared-for dining experience.

The restaurant's design is a triumph of style and atmosphere, offering panoramic views of London's skyline that include landmarks like the BBC Building, the Shard, Battersea Power Station, and the London Eye. The setting strikes a perfect balance between a tranquil retreat and proximity to the energy of London's West End.

The ambiance is complemented by modern lighting, decor, and music that cater to both city workers looking for a sophisticated night out and tourists seeking a special dining experience. Additionally, The Madera Restaurant and the Nest Rooftop Bar above offer private booking options for events.

The culinary journey at Madera is an exploration of Mexican flavours with a Californian twist. The menu spans from breakfast to dinner, with special weekend brunch options and even entertainment like fire breathers on select evenings. For pet lovers, the Nest Rooftop Bar's dog-friendly Sundays are a delightful touch.

Our dining experience began with tortillas and tomato salsa, an appetizing prelude to the feast that awaited. The beef barbacoa was a standout, offering a symphony of flavours that were both bold and well-balanced. The interactive sirloin hot rock dish allowed us to cook our meat to perfection right at our table—a delightful touch. The Mexican Fattoush salad and king prawn taqueria were not only visually striking but also packed with taste.

No Mexican dining experience would be complete without margaritas, and Madera's hibiscus and passion fruit versions were exceptional—both in flavour and potency.

It was evident that the staff took great pride in delivering an unparalleled "treehouse experience." A heartfelt thanks to Lawrence and his team for not just an exquisite meal, but for the personal tour of the restaurant and rooftop bar which offered breath-taking views.

The Madera Restaurant is not just about dining; it's about an experience—one that I would highly recommend to anyone looking for a unique escape in the heart of London.

FABER

FOOD: Exceptional seafood dishes showcasing fresh, high-quality ingredients, each bite offering exquisite and inventive flavours that leave a lasting impression.

VIEW: Elegant decor creates a visually stunning ambiance, enhancing the dining experience and offering a delightful, light-flooded space near Hammersmith station.

SERVICE: Attentive and knowledgeable staff provide impeccable service, ensuring every guest feels welcomed and well-cared for throughout their dining journey.

ATMOSPHERE: Warm and inviting, the restaurant blends sophistication with comfort, making it a perfect haven for an exceptional dining experience.

PHOTO: Exquisite seafood, elegant ambiance, and impeccable service await you at Faber Wine & Seafood, Hammersmith's hidden gem.

A Journey Through Faber
Wine & Seafood Restaurant

BY GENEVIEVE GRANT

" Indulge in the culinary brilliance of Faber Wine & Seafood Restaurant, a hidden gem near Hammersmith station. Led by Chef Ollie Bass, the menu dazzles with inventive seafood dishes, each bursting with freshness and flavor. An exceptional dining experience awaits, promising culinary bliss with every bite.

Nestled just a stone's throw away from Hammersmith station, Faber Wine & Seafood Restaurant is a hidden gem awaiting discovery. Despite its elegant decor, don't be misled into thinking this is a place exclusively for the elite; it's a welcoming haven for anyone seeking an exceptional dining experience. From the moment you step inside, the ambiance envelops you, setting the stage for a culinary journey that celebrates the bounties of the British Isles.

Faber Wine & Seafood is a welcoming spot offering exquisite, inventive seafood dishes with fresh, high-quality ingredients, all set in a beautifully elegant decor.

Led by the talented chef Ollie Bass, the menu boasts an array of seafood delicacies that are as exquisite as they are inventive. Each dish showcases the freshness and quality of the ingredients, leaving a lasting impression on even the most discerning palate. From the delicate Maldon oysters to the indulgent cuttlefish Bolognese, every bite is a revelation.

You might think from the elegant decor that the light-flooded restaurant caters for elites, and the menu is out of your reach, or even too complex for a simple afternoon of good eating. You'd be sadly misguided to pass this place by. Focusing on the gifts of the sea, and celebrating the coasts of these generous British Isles, the team at Faber have you in mind, whoever you are. Meanwhile, when you're ready for a piece of fish that's a reason to eat fish, Ollie Bass is here to show you just how beautiful a perfectly cooked piece of fish can be.

This review might become a bit repetitive, as we were gob smacked by the clarity of the flavours and the freshness of the ingredients.

We started with Maldon oysters, which were light, lush, clean seawater delicacies. The chalk stream trout tartare was a reve-

"Discover the hidden gem of Hammersmith - Faber Wine & Seafood, where every bite is a celebration of the sea's finest treasures."

lation. I've had some very expensive sushi in my life, and never tasted trout this… fresh. There's a richness in the dish that is accessed via the astounding clarity in the taste of the fish and the caviar. The chef's light horseradish cream simply presents the fish in its best light, without overwhelming it as some such sauces might. The generous burrata was absolutely silky, accompanied by samphire dressed with salty crunchy dulse crumbs. It's the kind of thing you've order just to see how wacky the chef is, and you might not expect it to work. But it does, dear reader. The only thing I'd suggest is a bit of bread to go with it, as the burrata is such a generous portion you want something to spread it on.

But then, if there were bread, you might not have room to really enjoy the rest. Asparagus tender and to-the-teeth with a spend wood cheese sauce topped with shaved cobnut, balanced in the varieties of subtle and gently weird palates – aspargus being a somehow stinky vegetable and the cheese's tang complimenting it perfectly.

Then we were delighted by a cuttlefish Bolognese on Coombes head farm sourdough. To think of making the most comforting of comfort foods – a Bolognese – with the most down to earth of seafoods – cuttlefish. Who is this mad genius? The smokiness and the headiness of the cuttlefish rested nicely on the dark spongy sourdough. This with a beer is the perfect lunch break.

For mains we had the seabass – Cornish, with wild garlic dressed Dorset clams, and mackerel with parsley-anchovy sauce.

If you like mackerel, you mustn't have theirs, because you will never be able to eat it anywhere else again. The combination of crispy skin and mouth melting flesh, the sauce that supports the glorious oily fish without argument, and the presentation. Well, we learned from our theatrically gifts server Tomas that Ollie went to art school. Of course, he did. The seabass as firm and fresh (there's that word again) and the clams were well-loved. In fact, we said to each other more than once, you can taste the love in these dishes.

A Culinary Voyage to South West Coastal India, Infused with Michelin-Star Magic

BY
KIRSTY
ROWE

"Embarking on a culinary odyssey at Quilon is akin to savouring the symphony of South West Coastal India on a plate – where Michelin-star excellence harmonizes with vibrant flavours, creating an unforgettable gastronomic masterpiece.

Located in the heart of London, just a stone's throw away from Buckingham Palace, Quilon Restaurant offers a gastronomic experience that's a harmonious blend of Michelin-star excellence and the vibrant flavours of South West Coastal Indian cuisine. During a recent weekend brunch outing, I had the pleasure of immersing myself in their celebrated Onam Brunch menu – an offering that beautifully captured the essence of this culinary tradition.

From the moment I walked in, Quilon's elegant ambience and attentive service set the stage for a memorable dining experience. The Onam Brunch, available every Saturday and Sunday, was an exploration of vegetarian and non- vegetarian delights from the region, each dish meticulously curated by the talented team led by Chef Sriram Aylur.

Sriram's lifelong passion for food began in his father's kitchen. Inspired by his father's joyful approach to cooking, he pursued culinary education, eventually joining Taj Hotels. After honing his skills, he opened the renowned Karavali Restaurant. He later established Quilon in London, blending traditional and innovative Southwest Indian cuisine. Quilon garnered numerous awards, including a Michelin Star, reflecting Sriram's progressive culinary vision and dedication to his craft.

The staff, as kind as they were knowledgeable, played an integral role in enhancing the entire experience. Each dish was presented with a fascinating introduction, delving into its origin and distinct flavours. This insight added an extra layer of enjoyment, allowing a deeper connection with the cuisine.

The Onam Brunch, both Vegetarian and Non-Vegetarian, bore the hallmark of Chef Sriram Aylur's culinary finesse. I delved into the Vegetarian Onam Brunch, a symphony of tastes that delighted the senses. The culinary adventure commenced with a sweet potato s-a-a-a-t, a harmonious blend of textures and flavours that left a delightful crunch. The water kosambri in a watermelon cup followed, a palate-cleansing marvel that was both fresh and invigorating.

The journey began with an assortment of traditional Indian snacks that included coin papadam, banana chips, jackfruit chips, sarkara varatti, chutneys, and pickles. This delightful array of crunchy bites provided a glimpse into the diverse textures and flavours that awaited.

The appetizers that followed were a testament to the restaurant's dedication to authenticity and innovation. The stuffed tapioca chop with its mint sauce was a surprising fusion of textures, while the banana flower vada paired with curry leaf chutney provided a tantalizing play of flavours. The mini masala dosa, served with sambhar, was a mini marvel of crispiness and spiciness.

The main courses were a true celebration of Kerala's culinary heritage. The kada chakka thiyal, a traditional Keralan breadfruit curry, showcased aromatic spices that danced on the palate. Olan, a coconut milk-based stew with black-eyed beans and ash gourd, offered a subtle balance of richness and lightness. Avial, a medley of South Indian vegetables seasoned with coconut, delivered a symphony of tastes and textures.

The erissery, pumpkin cooked with coconut and spices, was a comforting dish with a harmonious blend of flavors. Vellarikka pachadi, a Kerala cucumber raita, provided a cooling contrast. The beans and carrot thoran, with its mild spices and crunchy vegetables, was a perfect accompaniment to the flavourful coconut red rice and fluffy steamed rice.

The star of the show was undoubtedly the malabar paratha – a flaky, multi-layered bread that served as the perfect vessel for savouring the diverse curries. The meal concluded on a sweet note with ada pradaman, pal payasam, and pazam pori – each dessert showcasing the artistry of traditional Indian sweets.

Quilon's Onam Brunch is an exploration of flavours that transport you to the sun-soaked shores of South West Coastal India. While the dining experience is undoubtedly exceptional, the complexity and authenticity of the dishes might be better appreciated by those familiar

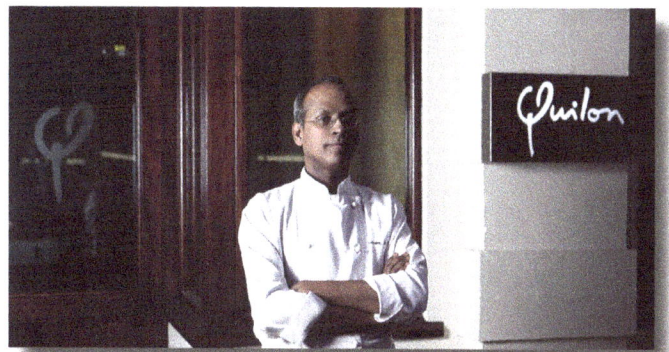

with Indian cuisine. The brunch presents an excellent opportunity to delve into the nuances of Keralan food, and with its stunning location and culinary prowess, Quilon is a must-visit destination for those seeking a gourmet adventure in London.

Quilon Restaurant is more than just a dining establishment; it's a sensory journey through the rich tapestry of South West Coastal Indian cuisine. From the serene ambiance to the knowledgeable staff, and most importantly, the tantalizing dishes crafted by Chef Sriram Aylur, every aspect converges to create an unforgettable experience. Whether you're a connoisseur of Indian cuisine or a curious epicurean, Quilon promises a culinary odyssey that's worth savouring. The brunch presents an excellent opportunity to delve into the nuances of Keralan food, and with its stunning location and culinary prowess, Quilon is a must-visit destination for those seeking a gourmet adventure in London.

Quilon Restaurant offers a Michelin-starred South West Indian culinary journey near Buckingham Palace, with exceptional service and exquisite dishes.

Quilon, nestled in Buckingham Gate, once hosted guests of Buckingham Palace and still exudes the elegance of those days with its refined interior and serene atmosphere. Executive chef Sriram Aylur brings to life the essence of modern southern Indian coastal cuisine, using the freshest ingredients to blend traditional home-cooking with contemporary dishes.

PHOTO: *A Festive Celebration of German Culture: Traditional Attire, Delicious Food, and Smiles at the Bar*

The Munich Cricket Club
Where Germany Meets London in Spectacular Style!

The Munich Cricket Club in Victoria offers an immersive Bavarian experience in London, with authentic décor and a warm welcome. The menu blends German and British cuisines, complemented by a variety of drinks. While desserts could improve, the lively atmosphere and themed events make it a must-visit destination for a taste of Oktoberfest year-round.

The Munich Cricket Club in London offers an authentic Bavarian experience with delicious food, lively atmosphere, and warm hospitality. Prost!

BY
LESLEY
MCHARG

"The Munich Cricket Club in London masterfully brings Bavarian charm with authentic décor, hearty cuisine, and lively events, creating unforgettable experiences."

When you step into The Munich Cricket Club, you're not just entering a restaurant; you're embarking on a lively, unforgettable journey into the heart of Bavaria. With three vibrant branches spread across London – Tower Hill, Victoria, and Canary Wharf – our recent visit to the Victoria location left us buzzing with excitement.

From the moment you ascend the stairs to the entrance, where an impressive display of German steins piques your curiosity, you know you're in for something special. Descending into the restaurant itself, the first thing that strikes you is the incredible sense of light and space, an unexpected surprise for a basement venue. With its high ceilings and unique lighting, The Munich Cricket Club successfully blends coziness with an open, inviting ambiance.

The interior design is a masterpiece of authenticity, transporting you straight to a traditional German beer hall. Wooden benches, long communal tables, checkered tablecloths, beer barrels, and charming wall displays adorned with beer labels and lederhosen create an atmosphere that is unmistakably Bavarian. It's as if Munich has been magically transported to the heart of London.

A highlight of our visit was the warm and friendly welcome we received from Florian, the General Manager, and his staff, all dressed in traditional German/Bavarian costumes. Their goal is clear: to recreate the spirit of Germany's Oktoberfest year-round while infusing it with the best of British hospitality. And thus, The Munich Cricket Club was born.

The menu is a tantalizing fusion of German and British delights. There's a wide selection of drinks, including flavored schnapps and a beer taster board for the beer enthusiasts among us. The cocktails, with their contemporary German twist, are a must-try. We couldn't get enough of the Apple Strudel Martini and the cheekily named German Pornstar. The food is a hearty affair with generous portions, featuring classics like goulash, noodles, schnitzel, currywurst, and sauerkraut. It's a culinary journey that transports your taste buds straight to Germany, right in the heart of bustling London.

While most dishes delighted our palates, we couldn't help but feel that the desserts, especially the apple strudel and German cheesecake, had room for improvement.

The Munich Cricket Club is not just a restaurant; it's an experience. It's the perfect spot for weekend brunches, post-work happy hour drinks, hen dos, stag dos, and private parties with two dedicated function areas. And the exciting news is that three branches are already lighting up London, with a fourth on the horizon.

The only disappointment of our visit? Missing out on the Thursday night extravaganza featuring live music, Oompah Bands, and the joy of dancing on the tables. Next time, we won't make that mistake. The Munich Cricket Club beckons with its promise of unbridled fun, delicious fare, and an atmosphere that transports you to the heart of Bavaria. Prost!

MACELLAIO RC

A Theatrical Dining Experience

FOOD: Perfectly grilled meats that melt in your mouth, with a focus on quality and flavor. A true carnivore's delight.

ATMOSPHERE: Theatrical and vintage Italian decor create a warm, welcoming vibe, perfect for pre-theatre dining and people-watching in Soho

SERVICE: Attentive and welcoming staff, even when understaffed, ensuring a pleasant dining experience with quick issue resolution.

PRICE: Reasonable prices for the quality of food and experience, making it a great value for meat lovers seeking a memorable meal.

PHOTO: Fiordilatte ice cream being prepared with olive oil and salt for a surprisingly delicious dessert.

MACELLAIO RC
A Carnivore's Delight in the Heart of Soho

BY
STORM | GIULIA CARLA
GREENWOOD | ROSSI

" Macellaio RC offers a pre-theatre dining spot with theatre-themed decor, vintage Italian charm, and a central grill showcasing the art of meat preparation.

Macellaio RC is Italian for butcher and the clue is in the name— this is the place you go for delicious cuts of perfectly grilled meat. Nested between the West End's hottest bills, theatre is all around you at this Soho restaurant. From the theatre posters adorning the walls and the artfully arranged meat counter and central grill, to the circus of Soho unfolding outside the open doors, this would be a perfect pre-theatre dining spot.

The decor is theatre-themed mixed with a vintage Italian feel. The wood panelling throughout gave it a warm, welcoming vibe and the display cases of meat made it clear this was a place for carnivores. The menu was styled to look like an Italian newspaper, the vintage fonts and cutouts of old Italian adverts between the lists of available dishes.

The majority of staff were Italian and all of them were very welcoming. Our waitress was especially attentive. The manager told us towards the end of the meal that they were understaffed that day due to illness, which made sense as the staff seemed rushed off their feet and the wait times for some items were long. We were also brought the wrong order for one of our starters, but this was quickly rectified and our waitress worked hard to make sure we had everything we'd ordered.

Meat was the focus from the start of our meal, as we were served a complimentary lardo candle with small slices of sourdough to dip into the warm lard. For starters we ordered focaccia ligure with stracchino (a type of smooth Italian cheese) and Parma ham and a vitello tonnato, which is thinly sliced veal with tuna and capers. The vitello tonnato was delicious, marrying the zingy flavour of the onions and the capers against the surprisingly delightful mixture of the tuna and meat. The focaccia was tasty, although slightly direr than expected and almost sweet to the taste. They had a nice selection of Italian wines and classic cocktails such as Aperol Spritz and Negroni. As we were planning to eat meat, we both chose a glass of red wine. We sampled both the Nero d'Avola and the Sangiovese. The Sangiovese was perfectly adequate, while the Nero d'Avola was surprisingly light for a normally bold wine and lacked the richness we were expecting.

Unsurprisingly, the meat is where this restaurant excels. The striploin and fillet, both cooked to medium rare on our request, melt in your mouth. The fillet was unbelievably tender, while every bite of the striploin packed a flavourful punch. Both were oiled and salted to perfection. It was also a nice touch to be able to watch them being cooked on the grill in the centre of the restaurant. To accompany our steaks we ordered two sides: parmesan and truffle chips and a green salad. The green salad was an unremarkable gem lettuce, but the dressing was good and the warm parmesan and truffle chips were thin cut, ridged and crunchy – the love child of chips and crisps. The smell of the truffle oil wafted towards us as they were brought to the table and the parmesan, slightly warmed by the heat of the chips, added another dimension.

To finish the meal we elected to try the tiramisù and ice cream. The tiramisù was good and had a tasty mascarpone cream, although the sponge was a little dry and would have benefitted from a little more of a coffee soak. The ice cream was prepared on a cart next to the table, as the waitress added oil from Taggiasca olives and salt to the ice cream dish. The contrast between the sweet ice cream and the tangy olive oil was surprisingly delicious and the theatre of the service added a nice touch.

We had a good evening dining at Macellaio RC. The atmosphere is fun and there's plenty of people watching to be done. The slightly lacklustre starters were saved by the delicious meat. If you're a voracious carnivore like us, this is the perfect place for a steak.

> **Macellaio excels in delivering perfectly grilled meats in a warm, theatrical setting, making it a must-visit for meat lovers.**

> **Macellaio, A Carnivore's oasis nestled in the heart of Soho, where vintage Italian charm meets theatrical dining.**

SHOZNA

A Culinary Jewel in Rochester

FOOD: The menu at Shozna is a delightful exploration of the Indian subcontinent's rich culinary heritage. Each dish, from the succulent Lamb and Chicken Tikka to the signature Karahi Mughal Special and Jaipuri Lamb, is a testament to Chef Jamal's exceptional skills and unique touches.

ATMOSPHERE: The restaurant boasts a modern, simplistic design with imaginative layouts and captivating lighting. The addition of large lamps, a modern bar, and a bowl filled with floating flowers and candles creates a warm, inviting environment.

SERVICE: The service was impeccable, with a keen attention to detail and a genuine desire to ensure a delightful dining experience. Chef Jamal's personal engagement with his guests adds a special touch, making patrons feel valued and welcomed.

PRICE: The overall value for money is excellent, considering the high standards maintained throughout.

PHOTO: Shozna is An Award-Winning Indian & Bangladeshi Restaurant in Rochester, Kent.

Exploring Authentic Flavours with Chef Jamal Ahmed

BY FATIH ONCU

"

Shozna in Rochester, Kent, offers exceptional Indian and Bangladeshi cuisine crafted by award-winning Chef Jamal "Jay" Ahmed, providing a memorable dining experience with top-notch service and a welcoming atmosphere.

I recently had the pleasure of dining at Shozna, a charming Indian and Bangladeshi restaurant nestled in Rochester, Kent. The restaurant's modern UK façade, adorned with a striking billboard and a quaint garden at the entrance, immediately set a welcoming tone.

Since its inception in Strood in 1996 and subsequent relocation to Rochester nearly two decades ago, Shozna has garnered an impressive array of national and international accolades. This success is a testament to the dedication and culinary prowess of Owner-Chef Jamal "Jay" Ahmed, who named the restaurant after his sister. Chef Jamal's unique touch to traditional curry dishes is evident in every bite.

George Shaw, food critique writer of Taste Lononn and I were warmly greeted by Chef Jamal upon arrival. Despite it being a mid-week evening, the restaurant was bustling, a clear indicator of its popularity. Remarkably, Chef Jamal has cultivated a loyal customer base of over 2,000 patrons, with 40% hailing from Rochester and 60% from surrounding towns.

Shozna delivers outstanding Indian and Bangladeshi dishes with impeccable service, making it a must-visit culinary destination in Rochester.

Chef Jamal invited us to the second floor, which is reserved for business meetings and special events with a capacity of 60 diners. Both the main dining area and the event space are impeccably designed, featuring a modern, simplistic aesthetic with imaginative layouts and captivating lighting.

Our evening began with Chef Jamal sharing his inspirational journey from Birmingham to London at the age of 16. After partnering in a restaurant in 1989, he amassed extensive experience and knowledge in Indian and Bangladeshi cuisine, culminating in the establishment of Shozna in 1996. Over the years, he has invested £600,000 in designing the restaurant, which boasts large lamps, a modern bar, and a stunning bowl filled with floating flowers and candles.

Shozna offers a rich culinary experience, showcasing the diverse flavours of the Indian subcontinent. The menu highlights regional variations, from the fish-rich dishes of Bangladesh to the spicier meat dishes of South India and Pakistan. Each dish is a testament to authentic Indian cooking, an art refined over generations.

Our culinary journey began with Lamb and Chicken Tikka, each priced at £5.90. These dishes provided a delightful burst of flavour with tender, marinated meat cooked to perfection. The smoky, spicy notes perfectly complemented the succulent texture, making them a must-try for any Indian cuisine enthusiast.

For the main course, we savoured the Karahi Mughal Special, Bengal Bemisal, Vegetable Balti, Jaipuri Lamb, and Curry Meat. The Karahi Mughal Special, priced at £13.90, featured boneless tandoori chicken with king prawn cooked with minced lamb in creamy special spices, served with pilau rice. This dish stood out with its rich, intricate flavours.

The Bengal Bemisal, at £17.90, offered a unique experience with Bengal fish fried in olive oil, cooked in medium spice and fresh herbs, and served with onion rice. This dish maintained the delicate flavour of the fish while introducing a delightful spice blend.

The Jaipuri Lamb, priced at £10.90, was a semi-dry dish prepared with spring onions, green peppers, and fresh herbs, offering a special recipe from Jaipur with a Madras hot twist. These main courses, each a signature creation by Chef Jamal, showcased his exceptional culinary talent.

To complement the meal, I chose a cocktail made with pineapple and lemon juice, which was refreshing and perfectly balanced.

Shozna offers a superb dining experience with a rich variety of exquisite dishes, impeccable service, and a warm, inviting atmosphere. Chef Jamal's passion for culinary excellence shines through in every aspect of the restaurant, making Shozna a must-visit destination for lovers of Indian and Bangladeshi cuisine.

Chef Jamal Ahmed, the mastermind behind Shozna's award-winning cuisine, sharing his inspirational journey and culinary expertise with guests.

Royal China

Exquisite Flavours and Elegant Ambiance

BY
FIONA HO
PERKINS

" Royal China offers an elegant ambiance and impeccable service. Starters were exquisite, especially the Golden Crispy Tofu. Chef's specials impressed, with flavorful Sichuan influences. Desserts provided a perfect finish. Overall, a delightful culinary journey.

On a dark and wet evening, we received a warm greeting from Jenny at the reception. Our table was set nicely by the window to allow us to enjoy the riverside view. The restaurant is decently sized, seating around 100-120 people, with a reception and bar area, and an open plan dining area. We were informed that a private room is available and can accommodate around 30 people.

It is decorated with dark wooden tables and chairs with gold dragons on the seat backs, well-matched with vibrant and textured green cushions. Wooden panelled walls display mountain scenery, while warm and angular lights hang from a ceiling decorated with a beautiful gold wooden dragon at the centre of the room. Splash windows are on the right side of the restaurant, making the room seem more spacious. Their wine cupboard/fridge display appeared full, with a good worldwide selection.

Overall, the restaurant decoration sings, creating a classy, tasteful, cosy atmosphere, which we thoroughly enjoyed throughout our visit.

After being seated, Jenny offered us a pot of hot jasmine tea to warm us up from the cold, which the staff continually kept up throughout our visit.

We ordered two cocktails, a lychee-based one and a spicy rum-based cocktail, which we were informed were very popular. They looked stunning, and were also refreshing, taking our minds off the wet weather. After a sip we could not wait to order some starters.

The assistant manager (Kenny) recommended the Golden Crispy Tofu to start which we selected along with Deep-fried Baby Squid with Spicy Salt and the Baked Pork Chop with Mandarin Sauce.

We could already smell the fragrance of the natural ingredients, fresh herbs, spices from the food in the restaurant, adding to the anticipation while we waited for our own order. When it arrived after a short while we are more than ready to start our East Asian culinary tasting journey. The presentation of the food looked good and was improved by their seemingly unique and differing serving dishes.

The Golden Crispy Tofu was prepared into small bite-sized cubes, lightly battered and crispy on the outside, while soft, smooth, and silky on the inside with a hint of spice. Dipping each cube into a sweet chilli sauce was a match made in heaven. We simply could not stop eating this dish! My dinner guest normally avoids tofu, stating it is too boring, bland, and tasteless, but Royal China's Golden Crispy Tofu is a game changer and will certainly change your perception.

The Baked Pork Chop with Mandarin Sauce is a Cantonese dish, the meat was so moist and tender, while the accompanying sauce was just right and not overpowering, reminding me of the tastes I experienced when visiting Hong Kong.

The Deep-Fried Baby Squid with Spicy Salt was also tasty, nicely textured in a light batter. However, while they had the right amount of salt, the spring onion and chilli lacked the kick I was expecting, making this dish the lesser of the three starters.

However, overall, the three starters were great dishes to accompany our lovely cocktails.

For our main courses, we ordered from their Chef Special Menu, which consisted of a variety of spicy dishes which are influenced by Sichuan cuisine. I am usually particularly cautious when selecting spicy food as I cannot enjoy food which is too hot.

We selected the Smacked Cucumber, Tiger Green Peppers Stuffed with Minced Prawns in Black Bean Sauce, and Creamy Beef Short Ribs.

The Smacked Cucumber was effectively another appetizer, but a welcome light, cold and refreshing dish with a zing from the chilli oil.

Tiger Green Pepper dish was exceptional with the combina-tion of the crispy texture from the pepper with the soft, spongy and meaty minced prawn, with just the right amount of spice to boot and the savoury black bean sauce coming through at the end of each bite.

The Creamy Beef Short Ribs tasted rich from the sauce, yet the taste of the smooth and tender meat was not overpow-ered at all. However, I would warn visitors to be prepared to get their hands dirty to get all the meat of the bone, or else consider asking for a knife and fork!

While we were well satisfied with our meal and the portion of each dish, Kenny surprised us with a cheeky smile and brought two desserts to our table, the Chilled Mango and Pomelo Sago and a Mango Pudding. They were lovely, refresh-ing, but not too sweet, making them a perfect palate cleanser.

In summary, we could not fault the quality and portions of the food nor the overall experience. The two menus (including the Chefs Spe-cial Menu) offer a wide selec-tion, which includes the dishes you would hope to find at your favourite Chinese restaurant while also offering some lesser known but very much authentic dishes for those who want a new tasting experience.

Furthermore, the customer service was welcoming, polite, and attentive, without interrupt-ing our enjoyment. Both Kenny and Jenny were highly knowl-edgeable of the restaurant and local area, making recommenda-tions for a visit during a warmer season. Whether you are looking for a meal for two, a family gathering, or a team dinner, you will not leave disappointed.

Royal China offers a delightful culinary experience with exquisite flavours, impeccable service, and an elegant ambiance, perfect for any occasion.

The Complete Guide to Healthy Drinks
By America's Test Kitchen

You'll appreciate knowing why our blends work and what each ingredient brings to the table.

ABOUT AMERICA'S TEST KITCHEN

America's Test Kitchen is well-known for its top-rated television shows with more than 4 million weekly public television viewers, bestselling cookbooks, magazines, websites, and cooking school. The highly reputable and recognizable brands of America's Test Kitchen, Cook's Illustrated, and Cook's

Your one-stop guidebook to healthy hydration with 160 recipes for expense-saving, sugar-sparing, all-natural beverages. It captures the test kitchen's discoveries and best techniques for juicing, brewing, smoothie making, fermenting, and more.

You'll appreciate knowing why our blends work and what each ingredient brings to the table. Try a zucchiña colada, lemongrass and star fruit infused water, and tepache, a flavorful fermented drink made from the rind of a pineapple.

Ferment the best kombucha, kefir, and tepache you've ever had

Make healthier DIY versions of beverages like V8® and Gatorade

Up your alcohol-free drink game with homemade low-sugar soda and seltzers made from fresh fruits and herbs

Mix your own loose tea blends using elderberries, lemon balm, echinachea, and more

Infuse coffees with fresh ingredients such as star anise and orange

Steep and simmer drinks like raw hot chocolate and switchel

Try unbelievably good juice combos such as parsnips and pears or sweet corn and blueberries

Customize your drinks with suggested ingredient substitutions to use ones you like or have on hand. Don't have it, don't worry!

Buy the best blender, juicer, or seltzer maker and use it with confidence based on ATK's reviews and tips

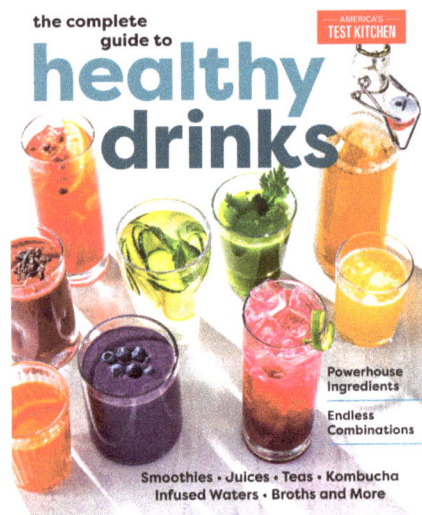

Paperback | $27.99
Published by America's Test Kitchen
Dec 13, 2022 | 272 Pages | 7-7/8 x 9-5/8 | ISBN 9781954210202

Everyday Bread
By America's Test Kitchen

Simplify the baking equation to add up to bread, of all kinds, on any schedule, as often as every day.

ABOUT AMERICA'S TEST KITCHEN

America's Test Kitchen is well-known for its top-rated television shows with more than 4 million weekly public television viewers, bestselling cookbooks, magazines, websites, and cooking school. The highly reputable and recognizable brands of America's Test Kitchen, Cook's Illustrated, and Cook's

Introducing the only cookbook to put homemade bread and convenience in the same sentence—whether you're a beginner baker or an enthusiast. Learn seven core recipes and then manipulate them into different shapes and flavors with ease for tons of new breads. Fit bread into your schedule with flexible, customizable timetables. Maybe you're looking to get bread on the table tonight, or maybe spreading steps over a few days is better for you. Recipes follow both paths, with new, streamlined techniques, no specialty equipment, and even loaves with no yeast, kneading, or shaping. You won't believe the chewy, open crumb and ultra-crisp crust you'll get from no-knead Dutch oven–baked loaves, the ease of quick breads that come together with a stir, and the dinner possibilities for flatbreads of all kinds.

Bake fast with a lively new roster of quick breads: Three-Ingredient Bread mimics yeasted loaves with a simple stir. Potato Biscuits with Bacon are on the dinner table in an hour.

Master 7 core dough recipes and then remix with confidence: American Sandwich Bread levels up to loaves swirled with spicy zhoug, crusted with seeds, or shaped into multipurpose buns and bâtards.

Impress with our reinvented Rustic No-Knead Bread: You don't need experience to turn out a beautiful bakery loaf. Cherry-Pistachio Whole-Wheat in a few folds, anyone?

Get unbelievable crust and crumb with your skillet or Dutch oven: No specialty equipment in this book.

Make recipes straight through, or hit the pause button and return when it's convenient: Have warm Sticky Buns in the morning or Thai Curry Butter Fan Rolls with dinner, even on a Tuesday.

Make your daily bread do work for your weekly meals: Homemade flatbreads like Mushroom Musakhan win over delivery on a weeknight, rustic Spicy Olive Bread makes a topped toast lunch.

Learn what to do with all the bread you'll make: Toast it, top it, crouton it—bread has endless uses.

Hardcover | $35.00
Published by America's Test Kitchen
Mar 07, 2023
| 376 Pages |
8-1/2 x 10 | ISBN
9781954210394

PHOTO: *Indulge in the culinary delights of Cafe Pacifico, where every dish is a flavourful masterpiece crafted to perfection. Bon appétit!*

Mixed Flavours at Cafe Pacifico
Vibrant Atmosphere Meets Lackluster Fare

" Cafe Pacifico offers a vibrant atmosphere and exceptional cocktails, making it a delightful spot for socializing. The lively ambiance and friendly staff create an enjoyable dining experience.

> "Cafe Pacifico offers a vibrant atmosphere and exceptional cocktails, making it a great spot for drinks and socializing. The lively ambiance and friendly staff create an enjoyable dining experience."

BY GENEVIEVE GRANT

Cafe Pacifico in Covent Garden offers a lively atmosphere with Mexican vibes and an extensive tequila selection. While cocktails impress, food falls short with lackluster seasoning and care evident in details like dry rice and wilting salad. Despite friendly staff and welcoming ambiance, food quality disappoints.

We showed up on the small side street in Covent Garden to a lively place. It felt convivial, the music giving Mexican vibes and the din of the diners giving you the feeling you were in a neighbourhood local, but Mexican. I liked the deep blue colour used to accent all the vibrant Mexican themed artwork, and the many shields hanging everywhere honouring those who had joined the 1000 Club, which our lovely host explained was a club you joined if you had a certain tequila. If you love tequila and mescaline this is the place to be. There's a long line behind the bar of what I imagine must be every agave based spirit known to humanity. The cocktails celebrate tequila and mezcal, but don't worry if. that's not your tipple, there's lots of other options. For drinks we tried the Picante Margarita, which had a lot of heat, so be warned it's more than just a little chili on top. This drink is committed to it's fire. We also had the Bru-Goni, a nix of mezcal and Campari, wonderfully smoky and complex as you'd imagine. My partner and I have this think about nachos. It seems there's never enough cheese on them wherever we go in the U.K. So we had to see what their version was. And it turns out all the cheese that was missing everywhere

Cafe Pacifico's cocktails are exceptional, boasting vibrant flavors and expert craftsmanship. They truly elevate the dining experience with every sip.

else is on the nachos at Cafe Pacifico. The guacamole, which you have to order separately, was fresh with a nice garlic kick and reassuring lumps of avocado to let us know it wasn't from a jar.

We tried the slow cooked short ribs and the prawn and fish tacos. The meat on the rib fell off the bone, and was doused in a cooked onion sauce, It's served with tortillas, rice, black beans, shredded cabbage and a green salsa so you can assemble your own tacos or just eat the parts you like. Sadly, though it looked impressive the rice was dry, the meat lacked any seasoning to make it stand out, and the green salsa seems like it came out of a bottle.

The prawn and fish tacos were a bit better. The fish was lightly battered and nicely cooked, but the tacos were laid with a large chunk of pineapple that overpowered them. A pineapple salsa would have made sense, but I had to remove the large pieces to enjoy the rest of the tacos. The dish was also served with black beans and the green salsa, as well as what was a generous tenderleaf salad. I was looking forward to the salad until I recognised wilted greens in the mix, and had to resign to picking out a few reliable leaves before giving up.

Small details give me the feeling someone has given up. A visit to the toilets revealed peeling wallpaper, and the lack of care in the food. It's a shame because the place has a great energy and the staff seem friendly.

While we were there they staff sang happy birthday to a table near us, and I appreciated the way the staff and the environment make you feel genuinely welcome. I'd pop by for drinks with friends on a night out, but wouldn't count on the food to life your mood.

Discover the Culinary Mastery of Executive Chef Jiwan Lal at Babur

BY
GEORGE
SHAW

"Babur in Forest Hill offers exquisite Indian cuisine with modern twists. Chef Jiwan Lal's 18-year tenure has earned numerous accolades, making it a top dining destination in London.

Executive Chef Jiwan Lal, who curates an exceptional menu of authentic regional dishes, with modern fine dining twists. Oberoi-trained Jiwan has been at Babur for a mere 18 years of its 39 year residency in Forest Hill – only 10 minutes from London Bridge by overland train. Look out for the Bengal tiger on the roof.

The cooking style employs a delicate touch of spice, which allows the diner to appreciate the full natural flavours of high quality fresh produce.

Chef Lal's talents have amassed an impressive array of accolades, such as the Asian Curry Awards – Fine Dining Restaurant, Asian Restaurant Awards – Fine Dining, London Suburbs and Asian & Oriental Chef of the Year, plus leading guide entries including Michelin, AA, Good Food, Harden's and Square Meal.

Babur, led by Executive Chef Jiwan Lal, offers exquisite regional dishes with modern twists, earning numerous accolades and guide entries.

At mixologist Rupam's recommendation, I tried one of the 'warm weather' cocktails, a heady 'Currytini' of Bombay Sapphire Gin, dry vermouth and cordial, flavoured with a fresh curry leaf and green chilli (£10.50), while TGS had a bottle of the "rich bodied" craft lager from local Brockley micro brewery (£4.95).

To explore the depth of the kitchen skills, my lunch guest, tourist guide Simon (a pescatarian) and I opted for the two 5-course tasting menus (£54.95, £50.95 vegetarian, plus £31 with optional paired wines). There are also slightly cheaper 4-course options.First up was a defty spiced Swordfish tikka with onion and radish pickle plus a plumb fresh Kasundi king prawn with green papaya murabba. For non-flesh eaters there is a Crispy tapioca coated beetroot cutlet offering.My second was the deliciously moist Tulsi malai chicken tikka served with cottage cheese, organic green peas and kadai spices, which allowed the bird to shine through. The veggie option was a "delightful" Saufiyani paneer tikka, "ginger and almond undertones", mango chutney with masala puff rice.

The third course was tender and gamey Goat shoulder tikka with green tomato and aubergine mash served with a garlicky spinach, sweet corn, mushroom and chana dal. TGS very much enjoyed his Garlicky spinach, cauliflower and potato with a "rich, creamy" dal makhni and "bready" plain nan. Next up was melt-in-the-mouth Slow cooked mutton served in a clay pot, steamed rice with Chicken Chettinad and a rice pancake. This was counterposed by the "playfully light" Soya keema broad beans dosa, accompanied with contrasting "zesty" spiced tomato and "heavenly" coconut chutney.

Finally, the rich Black cardamom fig kheer was served with a tangy Raspberry sorbet and, nutty was the perfect finale to a truly exquisite feast.

To celebrate its 39th birthday, Babur will be serving a special 'Flavours of Maharashtra' (India's second most populous state) 'culinary journey' of regional dishes from 17th July to 15th September.

LAZEEZ
A Lebanese Culinary Gem in Mayfair

"

Lazeez, a quaint Lebanese restaurant in Mayfair near Selfridges, boasts intimate modern décor. Offering Lebanese tapas, cocktails, and attentive service, it's a family-run gem with community initiatives and delicious cuisine.

Discovering Intimate Dining and Community Spirit Amidst Modern Décor and Authentic Cuisine

BY
LESLEY
MCHARG

Lazeez Lebanese Tapas in Mayfair is a culinary treasure. With its intimate ambiance, exceptional Lebanese tapas, and warm service, it offers a delightful dining experience. The restaurant's dedication to quality, community involvement, and authentic cuisine makes it a standout. A must-visit for foodies and shoppers alike!

Lazeez Lebanese Tapas is a hidden gem in the heart of Mayfair, located centrally adjacent to Selfridges Department Store. The restaurant itself sits in a quiet spot yet is moments away from the buzz of St Christopher's Place a favourite for "foodies" and shoppers on Oxford Street.

A warm greeting was received by one of the waiters Amal. The restaurant is small but has an intimate, modern feel with seating for around 16 diners upstairs and 16 downstairs. It is decorated with wooden flooring and tables, the wooden panelling walls are adorned with arch shaped mirrors and unusual ceiling lanterns, the windows dressed with a splash of green foliage and the bar area with an unusual large array of teapots on the shelving behind.

The food itself is Lebanese Tapas Style. The food menu has a wide selection of hot and cold tapas, salads, mains and sharing platters – both for mains and deserts. The drinks menu is extensive with a variety of cocktails, softails, spirits, beers and Lebanese wines.

A busy family run restaurant established for 15 years now – Lazeez provides catering for private functions in its basement area – birthday parties and special occasions. A takeaway service is offered as well as dining in and a street cafe seating area outside too. Brunch, lunch and dinner options provided. The restaurant certainly lives up to its 5 star hygiene award with its high standard of cleanliness throughout and well turned out staff. The menu is presented in English with access to an Arabic version via a QR code.

The meal itself consisted of charcoal grilled Halloumi Cheese a tasty hot tapas dish and Lazeez homemade houmous and flat bread – truly delicious. Mains of Chicken Shawarma with touches of ginger and Lamb Kafta served on skewers with salad. All generous size portions with lots of flavour and spices and beautifully presented. The meal was accompanied by a Lebanese red wine reminiscent of a Cabernet Sauvignon and a lemon mint softail. Mint tea followed – a delightful palate cleanser with a side of baklava. And to finish a shot of Lebanese coffee served with dates. This coffee is certainly not for the faint hearted but a welcome end to an outstanding meal.

On speaking to one of the Managers/Chef Javier, he advised me that all dishes are made from scratch within their kitchen. Dishes are continually adapted to reflect the true style of Lebanese cuisine. Javier clearly had a great enthusiasm and sense of pride for the restaurant's dishes. Javier is evidently very hands on both in the kitchen and in the restaurant itself – a nice personal touch.

The restaurant offers 15 per cent discount to local employees from workplaces like Selfridges nearby who regularly attend for meals after work. Lazeez has also been signed up to the Felix Project since 2016 providing food for the homeless. A joy to see a business with true appreciation in giving back to the local community.

My only disappointment was to not experience a cup of tea being served from one of their numerous metal teapots. These brought back childhood memories of Aladdins Lamps. Perhaps on my next visit…..

A busy family run restaurant established for 15 years now – Lazeez provides catering for private functions in its basement area – birthday parties and special occasions.

LISSOME

Italian Excellence on Kingsland Road

" Lissome Italian Restaurant on Kingsland Road offers an elegant ambiance and exceptional Italian cuisine. Expertly crafted cocktails, generous starters like Adriana Burrata and Spicy Butterfly Prawns, delightful mains like pumpkin raviolo and their signature pizza, showcase their culinary prowess. Despite a weak tiramisu, the dedication to quality and service shines through, making it a must-return dining spot.

BY GENEVIEVE GRANT

Lissome offers an exquisite Italian dining experience with impeccable dishes, a cozy ambiance, and exceptional service. Chef Jimi Hajri's passion and expertise make it a must-visit culinary gem.

Jimi Hajri may not sound like an Italian name, but don't judge a book by it's cover. Or in this case, don't judge the cuisine by the cook's name. Since 1995 he's been working in foodservice, and all of it has been italian. Lissome is proof of his love of the Italian and his expertise in seeing it created.

We went to Lissome on Kingsland Road on a Wednesday night. The environment has a gentle elegance, velvet covered banquette with genuinely comfortable cushions, warm lighting that's light enough to read the menu without squinting, low enough bring a little romance to the experience. The music added to the effect, italinate jazz, soft crooning, contemporary and nostalgic melodies to warm you on cold nights.

We started with the Truffle Sour cocktail. If you love truffles, having a sliver of it right under your nose as you sip the mellow complexity of this drink will thrill you. There's a weird genius happening in the mix of amaro montenegro, truffle, and citrus. And its a sign of good things to come.

For starters we had the Adriana Burrata. The serving sizes of the starters at Lissome are just too big. If you want room to really enjoy your main, share one, or leave some on the plate. This is easier said than done considering the perfect creaminess of the burrata, and the impossible flavour of the beefsteak tomatoes. I'm working on a scheme to get hold of some of those tomatoes from his supplier. Great italian cooking is for me about starting with great produce, and finding flavourful tomatoes in December in London is an early Christmas miracle.

We also had the Spicy Butterfly Prawns. The sauce a rich tomato and wine gravy with layers of heat from different kinds of chili. The homemade bread that came with it gave more proof of Jimi and his team's high standards. I would have asked for more bread to make the most of every last drop of the sauce, but we were already feeling the need to ensure we had room for what was to come.

The raviolo of the day was pumpkin. Generously filled parcels lightly scented with nutmeg, in a lemony sauce that was just the perfect balance to the pumpkin. Sometimes a sauce that looks that rich and buttery just drowns out the pasta, but this was light and fresh, leaving us feeling satisfied without being overwhelmed by butter. The Lissome pizza is a great showcase for their pizza skills. They make their own dough, and you really can taste it. The toppings are ample and flavourful, framed nicely by the freshness of the woodfired crust. When it comes to Italian food, my partner is pretty picky. He's travelled all over Italy as a touring musician, and enjoyed home cooking and the best the locals have to offer everywhere from Trieste to Bar. The smile on his face as he tasted each successive dish reassured me that my assessment was correct. We had hit the jackpot.

The final test of the kitchen's abilities was one specially cooked Arancini. And it was perfect. Crispy on the outside, fluffy with just a touch of cheesy comfort on the inside, subtle and light as can be.

For dessert we had Tiramisu and Chocolate Melt. The tiramisu was so weak on coffee that we couldn't taste it at all, and to his credit Jimi gave it a good sniff and acknowledged the mistake, In the process we learned a lot about the process of making tiramisu. I would say I'll try it myself at home, but to be honest next time I want one, I'll just head over to Lissome. Though our wasn't perfect this time, I have complete trust that Jimi will make it right next time. In fact, when we arrived, he was having his dinner and testing the food, giving feedback and making adjustments with his kitchen. This is a restaurant that serves to high standards, while making you feel at ease as you enjoy the gifts of their cooking.

Of all the places I've reviewed this year, this is one of them I'll be back to for dinner.

Lissome's pizza is a masterpiece crafted in a brick and wood oven, delivering the perfect blend of crispy crust and flavorful toppings. Chef Jimi Hajri's dedication to Italian cuisine shines through every bite. A must-try for pizza lovers!

Savouring Authentic Chinese Delights at YEYE
Traditional Recipes with a Contemporary Flair

BY
KIRSTY
ROWE

YEYE restaurant offers traditional Chinese dishes with innovative twists. Warm atmosphere, friendly staff, and delicious dishes like teriyaki chicken soup and salt and pepper crispy squid. A must-visit spot.

The smashed lemon tea was a refreshing and delicious
The spring rolls were crispy and flavourful.
The chive and prawn dumplings were perfectly cooked and had a delicious fresh flavour.
The teriyaki chicken soup was light and refreshing, with perfectly cooked noodles and crispy sliced chicken.

In the bustling heart of London's vibrant food scene, YEYE's Noodle & Dumpling stands out as a beacon for those seeking an authentic taste of Chinese culinary tradition, with a twist of modern innovation. Nestled amid the cacophony of a busy market street, YEYE's second branch at 58 Wentworth St, which I had the pleasure of visiting, is a gem not to be overlooked.

From the moment you step inside, the contrast between the lively outdoor atmosphere and the restaurant's soothing interior is palpable. Warm lighting and spacious seating arrangements invite diners into a serene dining experience, a much-welcomed respite from the weekend market hustle.

YEYE'S passion for traditional Chinese cuisine is evident in their meticulous approach to crafting noodle and dumpling dishes. Their dedication to innovation is equally apparent, with the owner's specially created noodle recipes representing years of perfected culinary artistry. This balance of old and new creates a menu that is both comforting and exciting, promising a unique experience for every visit.

My visit was made all the more enjoyable by Hang, my attentive waiter, whose service was as commendable as it was friendly. His reassurances regarding my nut allergy concerns were much appreciated, with a menu considerate enough to cater to such dietary needs without compromising on taste or variety.

The culinary journey began with a refreshing smashed lemon tea, an invigorating blend of lemon, kiwi lime, and a touch of syrup—a perfect palate cleanser. The starters set a high standard; the spring rolls were a delightful crunch, paired impeccably with sweet chilli sauce, while the chive and prawn dumplings were an exemplary showcase of softness and flavor.

The main course, teriyaki chicken soup, was a standout. The noodles, years in the making, did not disappoint; they were deliciously accompanied by crispy chicken slices and a generous helping of vegetables. This dish is a testament to YEYE's ability to elevate simple ingredients into something extraordinary.

Finally, the salt and pepper crispy squid was an exercise in textural perfection. Lightly seasoned for that extra zing, it was an impeccable end to a truly satisfying meal.

YEYE'S Noodle & Dumpling is more than just a restaurant; it's an experience that celebrates the rich tapestry of Chinese cuisine while embracing the spirit of innovation. Whether you're stopping by for a quick takeaway at their original location or settling in for a full dining experience at their Wentworth Street branch, YEYE'S promises an unforgettable culinary adventure. For those in search of noodles and dumplings made with love and a dash of creativity, look no further—YEYE has you covered.

A Delicious Discovery Near Dalston Junction

Delightful Dining, Quirky Decor, and Top-Class Pizza

"

Gordos's Pizzeria, located near Dalston Junction, offers a delightful dining experience with friendly staff and authentic decor. The standout is its unique, quirky decora- tion. The food is exceptional, with perfectly cooked pizza and top-class tiramisu. The restaurant blends seamlessly into East London's trendy scene.

BY MAGDALENA WALCZAK

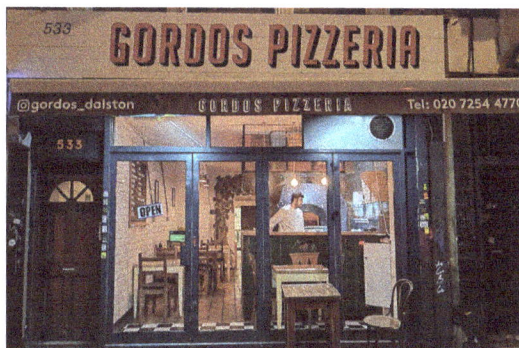

Gordos Pizzeria, nestled just a stone's throw away from Dalston Junction train station in the heart of a lively neighbourhood, offers a delightful dining experi- ence that's worth every visit. From the moment you step inside, you're greeted with a cosy atmosphere and friendly, smiling staff. The open kitch-

en, with its beautiful tiled oven, adds an authentic touch as you watch the chefs craft mouth-watering pizzas.

During my visit, I couldn't help but no- tice the bustling kitchen, with about four chefs working tirelessly to serve a restau- rant that was full yet managed to maintain a spacious and comfortable ambiance. The decor adds a charming touch, with custom water glasses and stylish ceramic plates, giving you the sense of a family-run estab- lishment with a quirky personality.

One of the standout features of Gor- dos Pizzeria is its unique and unexpected dec- oration, particularly in the restroom, where you'll find a focus on a rather amusing subject - pooping! It's an exam- ple of the restaurant's light-hearted and memorable approach to decor.

Now, let's talk about the food. My friend and I decided to share a pizza topped with olives, artichokes, and mushrooms, and it was an absolute delight. It was a harmoni- ous combination, and the pizza crust was perfect- ly cooked - reminiscent of the fla- vours and traditions straight from Italy.The simplicity of ingredients, the thin, brick oven-fired- crust,andthedelightfultomato sauce make it a true homage to the classics.

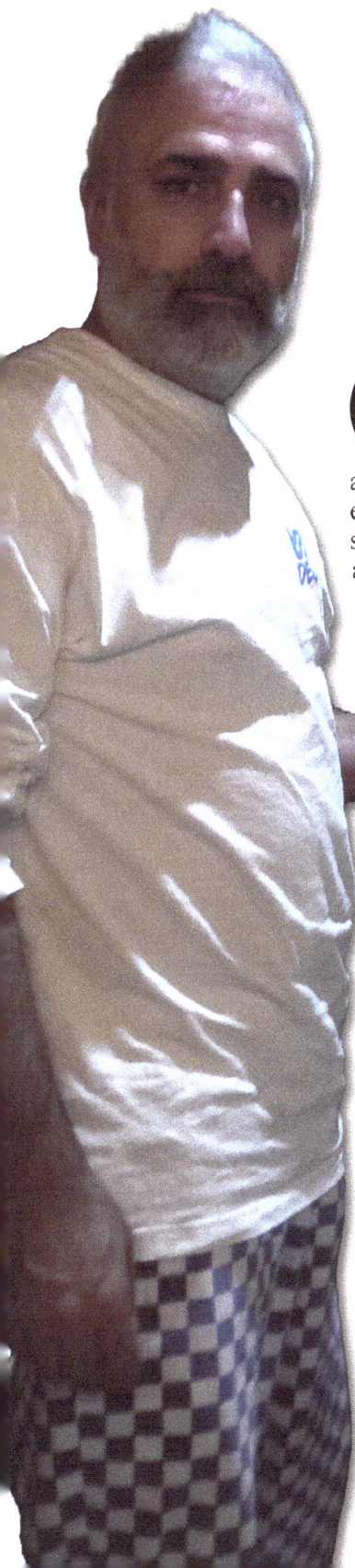

For dessert, we indulged in tiramisu, one of my all-time favourite treats. I've had my fair share of tiramisu, but the one at Gor- dos Pizzeria stands out as one of the best I've ever had. It was rich, creamy, and ex- pertly balanced in sweetness, truly top-class.

The atmosphere at Gordos Pizzeria is fur- ther elevated by the presence of a typical and trendy local cool crowd from Hackney. It's the kind of place where you can enjoy your meal alongside the hip and vibrant people of the neighbourhood. This restaurant seamless- ly blends into the Hackney scene, making it a hub for the stylish and fashionable crowd, giving it that authentic East London charm.

So there you go, Gordos Pizzeria is a hidden gem near Dalston Junction, of- fering a warm and inviting atmosphere, exceptional pizza, and unforgettable tira- misu. With its quirky decor, friendly staff, and the presence of Hackney's typical and trendy local crowd, it's a place that exudes character and deserves a visit for anyone in search of a memorable dining experi- ence. Don't miss out on this culinary gem in the heart of a buzzing neigh- bourhood.

Media, You and Your Business

BY
FATIH
ONCU

" *Effective Media Strategies for Your Restaurant*

I have been in the media for over 20 years and have conducted many interviews with authors, entrepreneurs, CEOs, artists, musicians, chefs and many others. All of whom are masters in their fields. I figured out something common among them; a strong relationship with the media.

Emma, Heathcote-James, Founder/CEO of the Little Soap Company, Winner of Queen's Enterprise Award 2022, was one of them. I asked Emma what was the secret of her success? Her answer was remarkable; "I say 'Yes' to Press! It doesn't matter what you are talking about – people will just remember you and the product. I would always say yes to News items."

Last month, I've had an ample time visiting some of the restaurants in Leamington Spa, England. It was a Tuesday evening. Business in restaurants were pretty sluggish that day, as it was early day in the week, and it would have been the same on Monday. These days are not good days for restaurants. Yet it was not the same for Giggling Squid, a Thai Restaurant in Royal Priors Shopping Centre on Recent Street. It was full and no available table for seating. When I entered the restaurant, I didn't ask to see the Manager, instead he started walking towards me with a smile. He must have understood that I am a journalist as I took a number of photographs of the outside of his premises. When he approached me, "Welcome, please let's go outside, and talk" he pleasantly said.

I had visited many restaurants that evening and all were very quiet. I was wondering about the crowd at Giggling Squid and asked the manager What's going on at his restaurant today? His answer was remarkable as well. "It's a normal day for us and our restaurant is full every evening. Of course our services, rich, tasty and diverse menu make us different, but beyond that, media relations has taken a part in our business. We have connections and communication with almost all media in Leamington Spa and surrounding towns."

Media has been a powerful tool to influence people positively and negatively. Today, we live under the power of media as a source of information, communication and entertainment that enhance the knowledge of us through the different types of news or events in our daily lives.

It is a communication theory that "if you watch television more

than two hours a day, your mentality would be televised mentality. You act and behave as you get form the television." This theory goes back to the 50s. Today our mind is shaped by the tools of mass communication, which consist of television, radio, newspapers, magazines and internet such as: Facebook, Twitter, YouTube, Instagram, Google and other social networking channels. It simply means that media has the power to give information and provide an easy means of communication among people. Media is a powerful and trusted tool among people living developed countries like the UK, US and EU.

ShenYun billbord ad, Mornington Crescent underground Station.

*"***** I have reviewed about 4.000 show, none can compare to what I saw tonigt."* – Richard Connema, Broadway Critic.

A billboard ad had covered nearly all of London's underground stations last year. Shen Yun has utilised media praise quote in their ad campaign during their show tour in the UK.

Let's look at the facts before we talk what to do;

FACTS ABOUT MEDIA

• 81% of consumers' purchasing decisions are influenced by their friends' social media posts. (Forbes)

• 66% of consumers have been inspired to purchase from a new brand after seeing media images from other consumers (Stackla)

• Consumers are 71% more likely to make a purchase based on media referrals. (Hubspot)

• Conversions increase 133% when mobile shoppers see positive reviews before buying. (Bazaarvoice)

• 78% of consumers say companies' media posts impact their purchases. (Forbes)

• 56% of consumers say they're more influenced by media images and videos when online shopping now than they were before the pandemic (Stackla)

WHAT TO DO?

Depending on your business, there are many ways to make your product, service or items.... News. Let's talk about a restaurant business for instance. You have a fancy restaurant, you're the only restaurant cooks and serves the steak, kebab and desserts. Yet many are not aware of it. Like many other businesses, restaurant business hasand parts; media relation is one of them. Here are some of the things you should do;

Web page. Having an attractive, professional website is the best way to stand out from the competition. A good effective website helps build a strong online presence and helps communicate quality information to not just your consumers but media.

Make your webpage media friendly. Your webpage should have a Press Room page which should cover Press releases , high quality images and recipes of some dishes you serve.

Press release. Write a press release whenever there is a reason to do so, like a grand opening, seasonal opening, new products, special items, services on special days, like Christmas, Father's Day, Mothers Days, Valentina's Day or any new dishes you just started serving.

Local Media. Search and collect the list of any local media and contact the editors. Invite them to your restaurant for some reasons like press conference, introducing your new dish, or something about your restaurant contributes such as an event, party or something like that.

National Media. Search and collect the list of national media, restaurant reviewers that specializes in restaurants and food businesses. If you are in the USA, contact The New York Times Restaurant Review editor if you are assertive about your cuisine, your services and the ambiance of your restaurant. Stay in touch with both local and national media editors and send them press releases occasionally.

ShenYun billboard ad, Mornington Crescent underground Station.

Reviews. Be active on review sites, magazines and newspapers. As Bazaar Voice stated that conversions increase 133% when mobile shoppers see positive reviews before buying. Media reviews are most effective tools to bring customers to your restaurant. Most customers read reviews before dining at the restaurant.

Grand opening. Organize a grand opening all the time. If you open a new restaurant or branch that is a good opportunity to invite media, local political figures, artists and some of your loyal customers. If not a new restaurant or branch, do a season's opening, celebration or find a reason to invite these figures. Or celebrate your restaurant's anniversary with media and selected royal clients.

Celebrate. Collect the list of local and national media that covers your interest or scoop of your area. Celebrating their birthday, Xmas day and so on, one might be a good reason to stay in touch with them.

Flat Earth Pizza uses the praise quote,get from Vogue magazine in their magazine ad.

Get Awards. Winning any credible award or receiving positive write-ups and reviews in newspapers and magazines is usually an indication that a business is committed to high standards. Such recognition can significantly enhance a company's reputation, showcasing its dedication to excellence and quality.

However, it is crucial to be discerning about the sources of these awards and recognitions. Do not seek or accept awards from individuals or organizations that sell them directly or through any means that could compromise your business's integrity. Awards that are bought rather than earned can damage your reputation and undermine the trust of your customers and stakeholders.

Instead, focus on earning accolades from reputable and independent bodies that recognize genuine achievements and contributions. This approach not only ensures that your awards are meaningful but also reinforces your commitment to maintaining high standards and ethical practices in your business operations.

Social Media. Social media is a part of mass media. Use and update them effectively. Social media has become the most influential and important virtual space where the platform is not only used for social networking but is also a great way of digitally advertising your brand and your products.

WHAT TO EXPECT FROM THE MEDIA?

Praise for Your Business and Yourself: First and foremost, expect praise for business and yourself. Receiving praise from the media can be a powerful tool for promoting your business. Just as Hollywood uses praise quotes to promote new films and actors, and theatres highlight glowing reviews for their plays, the same strategy applies to restaurants. Positive media quotes can significantly boost your business's visibility and credibility, making it easier to attract a wider audience.

A Good Review: Anticipate a thorough and positive review that highlights the strengths and unique aspects of foods and service.

Catchy Titles and Captions: Media features often come with attention-grabbing titles and captions that can draw readers' interest.

A Launchpad for More Features: Being featured in one media outlet can serve as a starting point for being featured in other media outlets. More features lead to more media attention.

Remember, while every business is unique, the key to standing out is to demonstrate your professionalism and the value you bring to the table. With a solid media strategy and the right tools, you can effectively boost your reputation, reach more clients, and significantly increase your sales.

ABOUT THE AUTHOR

Fatih Oncu is the founder and CEO of Newyox Media and the publisher of eight distinguished magazines, which are among the rare British magazines available in print in over 190 countries. With over 20 years of experience in the media industry, he has an extensive background in journalism, having studied at New York State University (CSR). He also pursued studies in Digital Publishing at NYU and Digital Transformation at MIT.

A Culinary Journey Through The Old Street Chinese

BY GENEVIEVE GRANT

Savour the Vibrant Fusion of Tradition and Taste in the Heart of Old Street

Embark on a flavourful adventure at The Old Street Chinese, where tradition meets innovation. Indulge in authentic dishes amidst a warm atmosphere, perfect for gatherings and culinary exploration.

Manager Haiyang Lu, also known as Hilary, has just returned to work after having her second child. She's warm and friendly, with a smile as generous as the portions at The Old Street Chinese. The menu is extensive, offering dishes from various Chinese regions. We were fortunate to visit on a Chinese holiday, and Haiyang kindly shared the story of the Dragon Boat Festival with us. More importantly, she guided us in ordering our food.

The Old Street Chinese is best known for its 'Chinese Spicy Pots,' featured at the beginning of the large menu. You can have it dry or in chili oil soup, and you can select from no fewer than 46 possible ingredients, ranging from konjac and sweet potato noodles to beef omasum, wax gourd, and quail egg. After selecting our ingredients for the Spicy Pot, we asked for further guidance and were recommended the more subtle Shanghai dumplings to balance out the experience.

The food arrived quickly. The Spicy Pot was served in a large communal dish and kept warm with a tealight. This meal is meant to feed a happy gathering of people. When they say spicy, they aren't kidding. Haiyang assured us that they adjust the heat level and the amount of Szechuan pepper (which gives a tingle to the tongue that borders on numbness) according to the customer's preference. If you like fish, definitely opt for the fresh fish in the Spicy Pot. The light breading melts in your mouth, and the fish itself is incredibly tender. Each ingredient was fresh and lightly cooked, allowing you to enjoy the different flavours in the dish. We particularly enjoyed the bright crunch of the Chinese cabbage and the wholesome bite of the generous portions of lotus root. The prawns were perfectly cooked, and did I mention the fresh fish? I'll be dreaming about it for days. The Shanghai dumplings were robust in their subtlety of flavours and sumptuous in the texture of their dough and filling.

The Old Street Chinese is scheduled for a remodel very soon. Currently, the decor features red cloth-covered tables and dark wood accents, with a full-length window that lets light in from Old Street. It's a little run-down, hence the imminent remodel, but perfectly clean, and I liked the down-to-earth, family-friendly atmosphere. There were flower garlands and other decorations for the Dragon Boat Festival, adding extra life to the place. Speaking of the festival, we were given a special dish made of sweet sticky rice and red bean paste called zongzi, made especially for the day. Haiyang mentioned that it's a dish being lost in time, as only the elders still know how to make it. People from the north prefer a sweet version, while those in the south enjoy a savoury, meat-based one. I enjoyed the smoky sweetness, which my partner likened to the taste of tea.

The Spicy Pots are great value for money, definitely meant for sharing with a few friends, and full of vibrant flavours and nutrition. When we first entered, I noticed that most of the other customers seemed to be Chinese, which I take as a good sign of authenticity and high standards in cooking. There are cosy corners and space for large gatherings, with a menu to suit all tastes and generous portions. If you find yourself near Old Street roundabout, drop by. You won't be disappointed. If you live or work in the area, this should definitely be your regular spot.

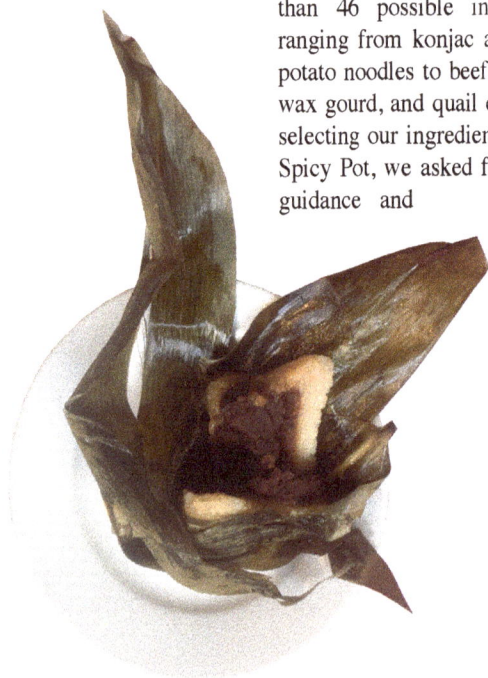

The Spicy Pots are great value for money, definitely meant for sharing with a few friends, and full of vibrant flavours and nutrition.

A Taste of Local Charm in Bethnal Green
ARCHES CAFE

" Arches Cafe, nestled beneath the train line near Bethnal Green Overground, offers a delightful blend of tradition and Turkish flair. From cosy interiors to authentic breakfasts and heartwarming tea, it's a haven for locals and visitors seeking a charming London experience.

BY
GENEVIEVE
GRANT

Arches Cafe, tucked away under the train line just a stone's throw from Bethnal Green Overground station, is a delightful hidden gem that combines the charm of a classic worker's cafe with a delightful Turkish twist. From the moment you step inside, you're greeted with the warmth and authenticity that's synonymous with local joints.

The menu, adorned with slightly faded photos of breakfast plates and easy-to-read large print, sets the tone for a no-fuss dining experience, perfect for the tired worker or the hungover local. The ambiance is buzzing with lively chatter, and the genuine smiles exchanged between the staff and the customers immediately make you feel like you're a part of the community. While the sound of trains passing overhead might not be everyone's cup of tea, I found it oddly romantic, adding a unique touch to the dining experience.

Arches Cafe has made an eco-conscious choice to keep the interior slightly cooler, which may not suit everyone, but it's commendable in these times of rising heating bills. However, the welcoming atmosphere compensates for any initial chill.

The Anatolian breakfast, ordered by my friend, was a delightful surprise. The succulent and slightly peppery Turkish sausage (sucuk) paired perfectly with expertly fried eggs. The magical touch of honey added an unexpected yet delightful flavour profile to the meal, making it a must-try.

I opted for the Spanish omelette, and it didn't disappoint. While it was a tad dry, it struck a good balance, avoiding the common pitfall of being overly greasy. The side salad provided a refreshing crunch and variety, complementing the dish nicely.

The tea at Arches Cafe is served just the way it should be, with a teapot containing two teabags, and plenty of milk on the side so you can customize it to your liking. As for my oat milk flat white, it leaned more towards a strong latte, reinforcing that this is the kind of place where a cup of tea is king. If you're on the hunt for the perfect coffee, you might want to explore other options.

And, of course, we couldn't resist trying the pancakes, which lived up to their American title with their fluffy and moist texture.

Arches Cafe exudes a sense of tradition and local flavour, with its malt vinegar on laminate tables and classic plastic seating. The Union Jack bunting in the window sets the tone for what you can expect from this long-standing establishment. It's a place where you'll find great tea, a dependable breakfast, and a warm and welcoming environment that makes you feel like family. Arches Cafe is a charming and unpretentious spot that captures the essence of a neighbourhood eatery, making it a must-visit for locals and visitors alike.

PHOTO: *Indulge in the exquisite flavours of Dorset Brasserie: a perfect blend of sweet and savoury delights, artfully presented to tantalize your taste buds.*

DORSET BRASSERIE
Impeccable Service and Cosy Atmosphere

Dorset Brasserie in London offers a warm, inviting atmosphere with impeccable service. Owner Remzi Kozhani's culinary expertise and Chef Sergio's global experience deliver unique, artfully presented dishes that consistently impress, earning rave reviews and ensuring a return visit.

> "Discover the charm of Dorset Brasserie: where cozy ambiance meets culinary excellence in the heart of London.

BY
KIRSTY
ROWE

Dorset Brasserie, near Baker Street, offers a warm ambiance, impeccable service, and exquisite cuisine. Chef Sergio and owner Remzi Kozhani create unforgettable dining experiences with their passion and expertise.

Tucked away on Melcombe Street, just minutes from Baker Street and Marylebone train station, Dorset Brasserie is a culinary spot that's sure to captivate your taste buds and your heart. Formerly known as Dorset Cafe, this cosy, clean, and spacious brasserie has recently undergone a transformation, and it's clear that the owner, Remzi Kozhani, and the talented chef, Sergio, are making waves in London's food scene.

Upon entering Dorset Brasserie, the warm and inviting ambiance instantly grabs your attention. The dimmed lighting creates a cosy atmosphere, making it the perfect place for an intimate meal, a casual get-together, or a leisurely afternoon escape. The large window facing the street allows you to people-watch while enjoying your meal, enhancing the overall dining experience.

Remzi Kozhani, with his extensive experience in the culinary world, has successfully brought the spirit of a European brasserie to London. Notably, Remzi Kozhani was the owner of the first food restaurant in Borough Farma Market back in 1998, and now, with the rebranding to Dorset Brasserie, he has taken his expertise to new heights. The commitment to quality and excellence is evident from the moment you walk through the door.

One of the standout features of Dorset Brasserie is their impeccable service. The staff is friendly, attentive, and well-versed in the menu, providing recommendations and ensuring a seamless dining experience. The owner's hands-on approach and passion for hospitality are palpable, which adds a personal touch to your visit.

Now, let's talk about the food. Dorset Brasserie takes your taste buds on a delightful journey. I began my culinary adventure with a vanilla hot chocolate, and it was the perfect way to start my meal. Rich and comforting, it was a great choice, especially on a brisk day.

The "Breakfast of Champions" was a unique and delectable dish that I couldn't resist trying. A warm waffle served with a poached egg, salmon, and melted cheese is not your typical breakfast fare, but it works wonderfully. The fine slices of avocado and the red and green mojo sauces from the Grand Canaries added a burst of flavours that beautifully complemented the sweetness of the waffle. It's a delightful combination of sweet and savoury that's a must-try.

For my next course, I opted for the chicken salad box, and it exceeded my expectations. The dish was brimming with flavour, featuring Mediterranean-seasoned diced chicken and chorizo paired with aromatic rice. The Greek salad on the side was a fresh and vibrant accompaniment. The slight kick from the spicy sauce and the richness of the halloumi cheese added layers of complexity to the dish. To quench my thirst, I enjoyed a refreshing blood orange mocktail that perfectly balanced the spiciness of the meal.

One thing that struck me during my visit was the attention to detail in the presentation of the dishes. Each plate was artfully arranged, demonstrating a commitment to not only the taste but also the visual appeal of the food. It's evident that the kitchen takes pride in every aspect of the dining experience.

Now, let's talk about the reputation of Dorset Brasserie. A quick look at their reviews on Google and TripAdvisor reveals a consistent pattern of satisfied customers. It's no surprise; I, too, had a delightful dining experience at this establishment. The combination of a charming atmosphere, impeccable service, and outstanding cuisine makes it a place you'll want to return to again and again.

Dorset Brasserie is a gem in the heart of London. Remzi Kozhani's passion for hospitality, coupled with Chef Sergio's culinary expertise, has created a dining destination that is sure to leave a lasting impression. Whether you're looking for a cosy spot for brunch, a romantic dinner, or a place to catch up with friends, Dorset Brasserie is a top-notch choice. With its inviting ambiance, delectable dishes, and attentive service, it's clear that Dorset Brasserie has raised the bar for dining in London. Don't miss the opportunity to savour the unique and unforgettable culinary experience it offers.

Available in
PRINT

The States to Australia Europe to Africa Taste London magazine is available over 190 countries and thousands of retaiers, platforms including Amazon, Barnes & Noble, Walmart, Waterstone's .....

ELECTRONIC

It is an electronic (flip book) format and interactive. Accessable from electronic devices like pc, smart phone, notepads..

ONLINE

All reviews and write-ups are featured online for free.

SOCIAL MEDIA

We are on Facebook, Instagram and X. Please follow us on social media @tastelondonmag

contact us today for an interview opportunity at editor@tasteof.london

TASTE
LONDON

A Summer Guide to the Best Bars and Restaurants
LONDON'S COCKTAIL CULTURE

MEDIA, YOU AND YOUR BUSINESS

OUTSIDE LONDON
SHOZNA

DINING DESTINATIONS
CHONGQING
THE MADERA FABER
QUILON
THE MUNICH
CRICKET CLUB
MACELLAIO RC
ROYAL CHINA
CAFE PACIFICO
BABUR
LAZEEZ

PIZZA
GORDOS
LISSOME

CHINESE
THE OLD ST
CHINESE
YEYE LONDON

CAFE
ARCHES
DORSET

Subscribe Now!

YES!   I would like a subscription to **TASTE** LONDON

☐ Current Issue for   ☐ Includes Shipping and Handling

☐ One-Year Subscription (_____ Issues) for

☐ Two-Year Subscription (_____ Issues) for

☐ I am a renewing a current subscription   ☐ I am a new subscriber

Name: _____   Phone: _____

Shipping Address: _____

Billing Address: _____

Email: _____

☐ Yes, I would like to receive updates, newsletters and special offers
☐ No, I would NOT like to receive updates, newsletters and special offers

Payment Type: ☐ Cash   ☐ Check

Please mail this form to:
Magazine Name:

www.ingramcontent.com/pod-product-compliance
Lightning Source LLC
Chambersburg PA
CBHW052348210326
41597CB00037B/6294